Tuppence for
Paper & String

Brenda is 92 years old and lives near Milton Keynes.
She worked as a Norland Nanny for over 60 years
and loved every minute of it.

Tuppence for Paper & String

BRENDA ASHFORD

HODDER

First published in Great Britain in 2013 by Hodder & Stoughton
An Hachette UK company

2

Copyright © Brenda Ashford 2013

A CIP catalogue record for this title is available from the British Library

Paperback ISBN 978 1 444 73991 6
Ebook ISBN 978 1 444 73989 3

Typeset by Hewer Text UK Ltd, Edinburgh
Printed and bound by CPI Group (UK) Ltd, Croydon, CR0 4YY

Hodder & Stoughton policy is to use papers that are natural, renewable
and recyclable products and made from wood grown in sustainable
forests. The logging and manufacturing processes are expected to
conform to the environmental regulations of the country of origin.

Hodder & Stoughton Ltd
338 Euston Road
London NW1 3BH

www.hodder.co.uk

Publisher's Acknowledgement

With thanks to the Hothfield History Society, Geoff Webb, author of *A Redbourn Commoner*, Katherine Stone of the War Studies Department, King's College London, Penelope Stokes, author of *Norland: The Story of the First One Hundred Years, 1892–1992*, published by the Norland College (1992), Susan Briggs, author of *Keep Smiling Through: The Home Front 1939–45*, Kevin Telfer, author of *The Remarkable Story of Great Ormond Street Hospital*, Richard Holmes, author of *Tommy*, and Doron Moraz and Zoe Thompson for their help and guidance on the Orthodox Jewish faith.

Contents

Foreword

This book came about (out of the blue) via the Norland College, at a time when I was getting very tired of being confined to my flat following a hip operation. I was asked if I was interested in writing about my time as a Norland Nurse before and after the Second World War. My immediate reaction was one of excitement, but I also felt very daunted at the prospect. I needn't have worried. Kate Thompson, whose help has been invaluable, came to see me soon afterwards, bringing her baby son Stanley, who was six weeks old. I had the privilege of giving him a bottle throughout our first meeting. Right from the start Kate and I got along so well together, and my sincere thanks go to her for the hard work, research and dedication to the making of this book. I am truly indebted to her.

I am grateful to my two brothers Christopher and David who have been so encouraging all along, and to the friends who have allowed me to write about the time spent with them and their families. We have changed names and some locations for confidentiality.

My sincere thanks go to my agent Diane Banks and the editors at Hodder & Stoughton. Also to the Norland College, for all their help, encouragement and friendliness throughout the writing of this book. Without them it would never have made it into print.

Lastly, but not least, I would like to thank the warden, Julia, and my friends at the sheltered accommodation where I now live; also my many friends in the Baptist Church where I worship, for their prayers, encouragement and support. Above all I thank God for his love and care for me throughout my ninety-two years.

Brenda Ashford

Introduction

The time is 7.30 a.m., the date is Christmas Eve 2012.

I smile as I pull back my bedroom curtains. A little warm glow that starts in my slippers soon tingles up the length of my spine. I simply adore Christmas Eve. No other day on the calendar promises quite so much joy, magic and promise.

Right on cue a light dusting of snow falls from the white skies and settles on the chimney tops outside. A breath of wind picks up a white feather from the ground and I watch transfixed as it dances, floats and flutters in the air.

'A white Christmas,' I murmur. 'How perfect.'

I know it will never be as cold or snowy as the winters of my past. I will never forget the snows of 1940. Do you know, it was the coldest winter on record? The snowfall buried cars and we had to travel everywhere by sledge. But still, even now, aged ninety-one, nothing thrills me like the sight of a white Christmas.

Hugging my dressing gown tight around me, I potter to my little kitchen, flick on the kettle and spoon tea leaves into a pot. While I wait for the kettle to boil I reflect on the day ahead.

With any luck my tiny one-bedroom flat will be filled with a steady stream of well-wishers, from family and friends to members of my church. I expect my kettle shall barely be off the boil as people pop in to share a cup of tea, drop off a card or simply pass on their season's greetings. I shiver with excitement. It really doesn't matter how old you are, the magic of the build-up to Christmas never fades.

I've baked, of course. Just a few mince pies, a pudding and a fruit cake. My shelves are also groaning with chocolate biscuits for eager little hands! Well, I have to have something to share with my guests young and old, don't I? Besides, I do so adore the rich, warm and spicy smell that fills a home when you bake.

Nothing says 'welcome' on Christmas Eve better than an oven-warm mince pie and piping hot tea in a china cup and saucer. And I want my home to be as toasty warm, open and inviting as possible, because what else is there in life?

After I have dressed and said my prayers, the warden, Julia, who looks after all the residents at the sheltered housing where I live, knocks on the door.

'Only me, Brenda,' her cheerful voice calls out. I fling open the door and shake my head. Even after all these years I still find it a surprise to be called Brenda and not 'Nanny'.

'Merry Christmas,' I cry, giving her a warm hug. 'And what have we here?'

'I swear you get more cards each year,' she chuckles, placing a thick wodge of cards on my coffee table. 'You could give Santa Claus a run for his money.'

'Oh thank you, Julia dear,' I smile. 'You will stop for a cup of tea, won't you?'

We share tea and swap stories and after Julia has left I pick up my cards and start to open them. Soon my eyes are filled with grateful tears.

Card after wonderful card from all my 'babies'. They come from all over Britain, but the senders all have one thing in common: they were all looked after by me, Nanny Brenda.

Dear Nana, we can't wait to see you at Christmas, hope you are taking care of yourself as much as you did us. Love Felix.

And another.

Dear Nana, we can't wait to see you. The spare bed is made up and the children have arranged some beautiful flowers in your room. Love Susanna.

And another.

To my favourite Nana, Merry Christmas. Have you baked my favourite chocolate cake? Love Jemima.

Gently I pin each card to the wall on a length of red velvet ribbon. Soon the walls of my little flat are covered with colourful cards from all my former charges, each expressing gratitude and festive wishes.

But it is I who should be thankful, thankful that I am in their thoughts. Each card is truly a joy to behold. For each and every single one of the 100-plus children I have cared for over the past sixty-two years as a Norland Nanny is very much in my heart. These beautiful children, who have blossomed into wonderful adults with lovely families of their own, have filled my heart and life with love.

Being a nanny, some might say Britain's oldest and longest-serving nanny, has been a privilege and an honour for which I count my blessings daily.

Opening the last card, I smile as I read: *To our oldest recruit, Merry Christmas, Nurse Ashford. Love from everyone at the Norland.*

The Norland College is where it all began, where I took my first nervous steps as a fledgling nanny back in 1939. What a wondrous journey of discovery I have been on since then.

Pinning up the card with the rest, my gaze turns back to the window and I find myself spellbound at the falling snowflakes.

Suddenly I find myself transported back to the magical time and place where it all began. Childhood. An innocent and idyllic place where love wraps you in a blanket of security, the world is such a big, exciting place, and there is always something amazing waiting to happen, just around the corner . . .

Are you sitting comfortably?

1

A Nanny is Born

> Hush-a-bye, baby, on the tree top,
> When the wind blows the cradle will rock;
> When the bough breaks the cradle will fall,
> Down will come baby, cradle and all.
> Seventeenth-century English lullaby

The world turns on tiny things. It's not the outstanding events that have influenced my life. Hearing we were at war with Germany, the devastation of the Blitz, the jubilant crowds on VE Day – these were all experiences I shall never forget. But for me, the single most life-altering moment was when I set eyes on my baby brother David shortly after his birth.

The build-up to this event had been momentous. Our house in Surrey had been scrubbed until it sparkled like a new penny. The oak floors gleamed like freshly churned butter. Every room smelt of lavender polish and carbolic soap, the leather thong handles on the doors glistened with beeswax, and pretty pink roses had been picked from the garden and dotted around the house in glass vases. King George V himself wouldn't have got such a rapturous reception had he showed up at Hallcroft House that sunny spring morning.

When my mother, Doris, had gone into labour I had been sent off to my aunt Jessie, along with my elder sister Kathleen, while my younger brothers Michael, Basil and Christopher were packed off to various other relatives. When the call finally came to say the baby had arrived, I was bouncing off the walls with excitement.

My father, Arnold, was duly dispatched to collect us all and bring us home. No sooner had the oak front door swung open than I scampered straight up the stairs like an overexcited puppy and bolted into Mother's bedroom as if my heels were on fire.

'Where's the baby?' I gasped, in a fever pitch of emotion.

An angry face loomed into view. Nurse Evans, the maternity nurse. The short, dumpy woman in her fifties, wearing an apron and hat, radiated disapproval.

'Hush, child,' she hissed. 'You'll wake the baby.'

But her words were lost on me. Because there, nestled in his little wicker Moses basket lined in mauve cotton and organza and delicate mauve bows, was quite simply the most exquisite thing I had ever set eyes on.

'Oh,' I breathed in wide-eyed wonder.

'Meet your baby brother David,' Mother smiled softly from her bed.

I swear my heart stopped in my chest.

David was just a tiny little scrap of a thing dressed in a white cotton gown, no bigger than a porcelain doll. Any disappointment I may have had over not having a baby sister melted away when he snuffled and sleepily opened his eyes.

This little creature fixed his dark blue eyes on mine and I was done for, hook, line and sinker.

'Can I hold him?' I gushed, utterly mesmerised.

'No! He's not to be woken,' Nurse Evans said sternly through thin lips from the corner of the bedroom.

But even a cranky old nurse couldn't stem the unspeakable joy that flooded through me.

Was it his golden lashes that swept over creamy cheeks, or the little murmurs and sighs he made when he slept? Or was it the way his tiny fingers curled round mine and the beautiful musky smell that filled my nostrils when I kissed his soft, downy hair? No, the thing I loved most about David and every baby I cared for after that was their heart-breaking innocence.

Adults are complicated, contrary beings, capable of hurting or betraying you. But babies are simple, sweet and full of love.

There is nothing in life I adore more than babies. Babies have a hold on my heart like nothing else and my life has been devoted to cherishing, protecting, nurturing and loving them.

A baby has a special way of adding joy to every single day and can flood your heart with love like nothing else. Uniquely vulnerable, babies are born with a need for love and never outgrow it.

How strange I find it when some people claim you can never truly love a child who is not your own. This defies every instinct that runs through me. For I have loved children born to other women all my life and yet never had my own family.

Many great things were invented and created in 1930, the year David was born: helicopters, FM radio broadcasting, the jet engine, and the world's first antibiotic to name just a few. But to my mind the greatest creation ever was my baby brother. Today David is eighty-three, and we still share the bond that I know was created in those precious early days.

From then on I cared for David as if he were my own. My mother had only to issue a simple request and I was on it. Nothing was too much trouble. I fed him his bottles, helped bathe him, changed his cloth nappies, sterilised his glass feeding bottles and spent hours singing him lullabies.

When he cut his first tooth I helped the pain of teething by giving him an ivory ring to chew on or dashing to the shops to buy him Allenburys rusks. When he was ready to be weaned, I was the one gently feeding him gruel, or porridge as we would call it now.

Most of all I loved gently picking him up out of his warm, cosy nest to feed him his evening bottle. So sweet and drowsy was he that his little rosebud lips would begin sucking before the bottle was even anywhere near them. Then, when finally presented with the bottle, like a little lamb he would hungrily latch on and suckle. I witnessed a small miracle every evening at 6 p.m.

That little boy flooded my heart with love every time he nestled into my chest and fell asleep on me, and when I gently put him on my shoulder to wind him and he gave a soft milky burp it did so make me chuckle.

Those days exist in my memory with a warm and rosy glow. Little did I know it then, but they sparked a lifelong love affair with babies and children. They were halcyon times, caring for my baby brother and living in our lovely home. Every day was filled with magic and promise . . .

If home is where the heart is, then the heart of my home was my parents. You'd be hard-pressed to find a more devoted couple than Doris and Arnold Ashford. I often wonder what the secret to their success was, but in forty-five years of marriage they could hardly bear to leave each other's side.

My mother was a gentle soul, a quiet, loving woman devoted to her husband and six children. Women had only won the right to vote in 1928, seven years after my birth, and traditional attitudes towards women prevailed. Married women were not expected to work. It never occurred to any of us that Mother should leave the home and actually get a job. Nor to my mother either, I suspect.

Mother was never happier than on the Saturday afternoons we spent in front of a crackling coal fire in the sitting room, with Henry Hall's BBC dance orchestra playing on the gramophone, accompanied by the clicking of Mother's knitting needles.

My mother had six children pretty much one after the other so she always seemed to be either pregnant or nursing a baby. But every so often my father would insist on sweeping her to her feet so they could dance around the sitting room.

'Dance, Bobby?' he'd smile, gathering her in his arms.

I often wondered why he called her Bobby. It was only years later that I discovered Mother had contracted Spanish flu before she had us children and was really rather ill. Spanish flu hit England in 1918, just after the end of the First World War. It was a worldwide pandemic and 50 million people died, making it one of the deadliest natural disasters in human history.

Poor Mother was so ill all her hair fell out and after that it never grew past her shoulders so she always wore it in a bob, hence Father's nickname for her. I thank goodness she was strong enough to survive – she was one of the lucky ones.

Maybe this made Father love and cherish my mother all the more. Their eyes would lock and they would smile tenderly at each other. It was a secret little smile of understanding and it left me breathless with wonder.

In forty-five years of marriage I didn't hear a single word uttered in anger between them. They set a marvellously good example by never, ever quarrelling in front of us. They exercised extreme self-control and courtesy. You must remember, and this is something my parents knew of course, that in little ones the imitative faculties are highly developed and a child's character will receive lasting impressions from those with whom he or she comes into contact.

In later life if I ever heard one of the families I worked for bickering I was horrified. Why would you fill your home with anger and subject your children to disharmony? It remains a mystery to me today. Maybe that's another reason I never married. How could any relationship match up to my parents'?

My father's eyes shone with love whenever he talked of my mother and she in turn devoted her life to him and us children. This intense love just made the tragedies that occurred later all the more painful.

It saddens me a little to think that I never found that love for myself, but I don't dwell on it. I prefer to think instead that the love they gave me enriched my whole life. Besides, I was too busy with my babies.

Doris and Arnold were so potty about one another they insisted on having every Sunday afternoon by themselves, with us children packed off to the garden. We knew better than to try and disturb them. I wasn't short of playmates, though. Besides me there was Kathleen, my elder sister by thirteen months, and my four younger brothers, Michael, Basil, Christopher and David.

The essence of my childhood was simplicity, and this is the key to any happy childhood. I remember reading this once in *Etiquette for the Children* (1901), and I passionately believe it to be true.

> *The simpler the life led by children the happier they will be. Simple meals, regular hours and plenty of healthful exercise should be the keynote of the regime for both nursery and schoolroom.*
>
> *How pleasant it is to see the enjoyment of children so brought up at the most simple treats and pleasures.*
>
> *They are real children in every sense of the word and in later life they will have none but happy recollections of a childhood passed in this way.*

Because my days weren't filled with television, computer games and constant activities, my siblings and I learnt to use our imaginations. Sometimes children need to be bored in order to stimulate themselves. Except that with five siblings for company, life was anything but boring.

Kathleen was the quiet, clever bookworm. Then there was me. Books and study weren't my bag, oh no. If there was a tree to be climbed, a stream to be waded through or a field to be explored you could bet I'd be there, in the thick of it with my four brothers, flushed with excitement. Why should boys get to have all the fun?

While Kathleen was upstairs with her nose in a book, I was usually to be found tearing through the vegetable patch with a headdress on, whooping at the top of my voice, pretending to be an Indian or a cowboy. Kale, cabbages and carrots were trampled underfoot as I ran hollering after my little brothers.

I loved our house, but as a child the garden was one giant adventure playground that fed my vivid imagination.

The rockery in the front garden, which was usually ablaze with colour, was not simply a place to cultivate alpine flowers. To me it was a mountain to be scaled, or an ideal lookout for a surprise enemy attack. The kissing gate at the end of a path lined with lavender was the perfect place to launch an ambush on an unsuspecting little brother. The rose garden at the back? Why a training camp for spies, of course. And the fields, or roughs as we called them, which backed on to our house, they were a wild territory to roam for hours on end, with streams to dam, blackberries to pick and frontiers to conquer.

My mother never worried about us when we played there, sometimes for a whole day. In fact she would make us some cheese sandwiches and pack us off out there, where we could be anyone we wanted to be, an explorer, a nurse, a train driver . . .

But the delicious smell of Mother's home-baked Queen's Pudding would creep out from the kitchen, over the fields and soon have us haring for home.

Poor Mother. Six grubby children would tear into the kitchen like a giant whirlwind, clutching all manner of treasures, from sheep's wool we'd collected from the fences to acorns and sticks.

'Eurgh,' she'd cry when she spotted the wool. 'Dirty things full of maggots and lice.'

I did little to trouble my mother. We left that to Basil, the naughty daredevil of the family. If there was trouble to be found, Basil would be there, in the thick of it.

It was Basil who coined the rhyme for little Bobby Penfold, the washerwoman's son who brought back our freshly laundered clothes each week, wheeling it up the drive in a baby's pram.

Washing's in the pram, baby's in the bath, Bobby pushes it up the hill, how it makes us laugh.

It was also Basil who wrote 'bomfers' on the coalhouse door. Bomfers was just a silly word that made us children roar with laughter as we imagined it to be something rather naughty. Whatever it was, it earned Basil a clip round the ear. If you heard a distant cry of alarm from somewhere in the house you could bet Basil had jumped out, shouted 'Boo!' and run away laughing.

We had no television, DVDs or computer games to feed our imaginations; we relied solely on our surroundings. Hallcroft, our childhood home, was a beautiful idyll that Father had worked hard to create.

Arnold Ashford was a six-foot-tall bear of a man. With his cheeky crooked grin, pointed ears and striking blue eyes that sparkled with fun, I worshipped him. His slight stutter and lisp just endeared him to me more.

From Monday morning to Saturday afternoon, Father worked hard all week in Regent Street in London, running a business supplying ladies' and children's knitwear to grand stores like Harrods. With six mouths to feed he was no stranger to hard work, but he earned enough to design and have built his dream home.

Work may have claimed my father for most of the week, but come midday Saturday he was all ours. As soon as we heard his key in the lock we jumped all over him like excited puppies. His smart tailored navy wool suit, tie, trilby and briefcase would soon be discarded in favour of fawn flannels and a cotton shirt. Then the fun would begin.

'What have you brought for us, Daddy?' we'd cry.

'Close your eyes and hold out your hands,' he'd grin, his voice rich with fun and laughter.

Eagerly, I'd squeeze my eyes shut and stick out my hands. Just the rustling of a brown paper bag was enough to make my mouth water.

'No peeking,' he'd warn. As if I'd want to spoil the magic of the moment.

Seconds later a pear drop or some other tasty morsel would be deposited into our outstretched palms. Mother was always rewarded with a bag of sugared almonds and a kiss on the cheek. For tastebuds unaccustomed to really sweet things, the tangy, acidic burst of flavour on my tongue was like nectar.

Pear drops were my favourite and always made a Saturday, but if it wasn't those it would be bullseyes, which we'd take out to the roughs and suck until our tongues were purple. Sometimes Father brought home Pontefract cakes, which were small liquorice disks, but I never understood how anyone could like liquorice.

I must confess Father's treats left me with a lifelong sweet tooth. If you were to visit me in my flat today you would find a good number of chocolate biscuits stacked in my cupboards. One bite of heavenly chocolate and if I close my eyes I am transported back to my childhood.

Father's attentions didn't stop there. Whilst some fathers may have retired to the study with a paper and strict instructions not to disturb, our father adopted a more hands-on approach.

We loved sitting at his feet as he read *Rupert the Bear* to us and supped stout from a large brown bottle. For us children it was a glass of milk, delivered weekly by a milkman on a horse-drawn float and sold by the jug from a stainless-steel milk churn, or, in the winter, a cup of hot cocoa.

On one memorable occasion Father spent hours outside in the garden plotting a surprise. By the time we children were finally allowed outside the suspense was killing us.

Father stood in the middle of the lawn to the side of the house that had always been earmarked for use as a tennis court, with a smile a mile wide.

'What are we looking at?' I piped up, puzzled.

'Look down,' he winked.

Looking down, we realised Father had mowed lines in the garden to look like railway tracks, and up and down the tracks he'd placed 'signals' that he'd made in the shed and operated with a string pulley system.

'Who wants to play trains?' he bellowed.

Did we ever? Every Saturday afternoon after that was spent hurtling up and down the tracks on our trains, which to the untrained eye might have looked like bicycles.

Mother and Father's unashamed love of children, enthusiasm for life and sense of fun made our childhood that much richer. Thanks to their efforts, I realise now that becoming a mother or father doesn't automatically make you a good parent. You have to learn and work hard at family life, a lesson I hope I have instilled in my many charges.

My idyllic childhood ended abruptly in 1932 when I turned eleven and was sent to Courtfield Gardens, a boarding school for girls in Bognor Regis, along with my sister Kathleen.

It was only 50 miles away, but I may as well have been travelling to the moon. Apart from our trips into the village I had scarcely left Hallcroft. But being forced into a regimented school routine taught me one important lesson, and in many ways was the catalyst for my becoming a nanny.

I was not academic. Not in the slightest. I could no more solve complicated mathematical formulas than I could speak Swahili. Unlike Kathleen, whose finely tuned brain seemed to pick up everything in a heartbeat.

Endless dreary lessons on algebra, freezing cold swims in the Channel and being forced to walk to church in a crocodile line whilst trussed up in a corset, wool stockings and petticoats, were enough to give one a lifelong aversion to education.

Salvation came in the form of the Norland Institute. Mother had always longed to be a nanny, but her father, my Grandpa Brown, had forbade it. In the 1900s becoming a children's nanny wasn't deemed a suitable career choice for a young lady from an upper-middle-class background.

Fortunately for me, Mother was more enlightened. After I dropped out of school aged fourteen and drifted through life as a mother's help for four years, she was the one who urged me to apply and who took me to the interview. I felt a lot of pressure on my eighteen-year-old shoulders to make a good impression.

I remember the interview like it was yesterday . . .

Alighting the train at Victoria, my senses were assaulted. I'd never been to the big city before and I was bewildered and excited by everything I saw.

Mother had decided we should walk from Victoria to the home of Norland at Pembridge Square in London's Notting Hill. There was intense noise everywhere. Red buses whizzed past belching out clouds of smoke, and the road seemed to be clogged up with motor cars and electric trolleybuses. We even passed an underground station, where, Mother told me, there was a train every ninety seconds.

Unimaginable, and so different from the sleepy Surrey lanes my siblings and I were used to meandering along. I felt so small. Everyone seemed to be marching about with real purpose and a sense of determination.

Soon the crowded cobbled streets gave way to wider pavements and smart leafy squares. Elegant white stuccoed mansions looked out on a slow-moving world.

Calm, peace and prosperity prevailed. Norland Nannies and smart mothers pushed their fashionable black coach prams serenely in front of the imposing mansion houses. Little girls in smart smock dresses walked in a crocodile to school; boys in sailor suits ran along clutching boats to sail on the Serpentine in Hyde Park.

My mother stopped in front of one of the grandest homes I'd ever seen: 7, 10 and 11 Pembridge Square,

London W2. Home of the Norland Institute Nurseries Ltd.

I felt like a little mouse on the doorstep. I'd never crossed the threshold of somewhere so grand.

Mother knocked on the imposing black door.

Looking back, it must have been a strange moment for her. She too had longed to train with the Norland. Times had changed and there I was, about to have the interview she had always longed to have.

Mother turned to me with a faraway look in her eyes. Excitement and something else, sadness perhaps, flickered over her beautiful face.

'I can't tell you how much I would love to have been a Norland Nanny, Brenda,' she said softly. 'I loved babies just as much as you.'

I didn't doubt it. She would have made a wonderful nanny; no one knew more about children than my mother.

She shook herself a little, as if to shrug off the ghosts of unchased dreams. 'Listen to me,' she snorted as the door swung open. 'I'm so thrilled for you, darling. Let's show them what you're made of.'

Straightening out my coat and smoothing down a stray hair, she pushed me gently inside the impressive hallway.

A few chairs lined the black and white tiled corridor. Mother and I sat down nervously. On the wall a large clock ticked ominously.

Finally a door was flung open and a tall, imposing woman I guessed to be in her forties towered over us. She was dressed immaculately in a dark-coloured dress with collar and cuffs trimmed in white lace.

Miss Ruth Whitehead. The principal, and to my young mind a truly terrifying sight. This woman held the key to my future.

'I'll have a word with you now,' she said.

Mother and I leapt to our feet, scraping back our chairs and nervously straightening our skirts.

'Not you,' she said, fixing my mother with a penetrating gaze. 'You stay here.'

Mother sat down, well and truly put in her place.

My heart hammering, I followed Miss Whitehead into her office and sat down opposite her, on the other side of a grand mahogany desk. On the wall behind her head was a black and white photo of a regal-looking lady underneath the Norland motto: 'Love Never Faileth'. She seemed to be staring straight at me.

'Emily Ward, our founder,' said Miss Whitehead as her eyes followed my gaze.

I listened intently as Miss Whitehead filled me in on the history of the Norland.

In 1892, inspired by the alternative theories of teacher Friedrich Froebel, who likened children to plants that needed nurture and love in order to flourish, Emily Ward set up a training institute for ladies 'of genteel birth' to become nannies. Her aim was to overthrow the tyranny that ruled in Victorian nurseries and train nannies who rejected spanking in favour of love and encouragement to raise children.

On hearing the inspiring story of Emily Ward's life's work, my heart felt like it was about to burst. I practically shot out of my seat as excitement bubbled over.

'But this is me,' I blurted. 'This is the way I feel about children.'

I felt like the sun had just come out from behind the clouds. The world was suddenly a far, far bigger place than Surrey. Sitting in that smart London house I had an epiphany, a lightbulb moment if you like.

Becoming a Norland Nanny was my calling in life.

I wasn't clever enough to be a teacher or a nurse, like Kathleen was training to be, but I did love babies and children. If Norland was a glove, then it fitted me perfectly. I too could help bring the dreams of children to life. I could love, cherish, protect and care for a baby with more heartfelt passion than anyone I knew. To nurture a baby, to help it on its journey into adulthood, was an honour and a privilege as far as I was concerned.

Despite my rattling nerves, Miss Whitehead accepted me as a student and even granted me a bursary to fund the cost of my training. Her faith in me was a turning point in my life. Often our lives and destinies are shaped by an invisible hand, strange forces out of our control, but that redoubtable lady's decision to welcome me into the Norland fold changed the direction of my life for ever.

The crisp spring morning of 23 March 1939 was the first day of the rest of my life. It was the day I began my training at the Norland Institute, fizzing over with youthful energy and enthusiasm to cram my brain with as much childcare knowledge as I possibly could.

As I set down my case on the parquet flooring of the dormitory at the Norland HQ, I kissed goodbye to the old me, a directionless, confused young girl, and welcomed into the world a new me. A smart young recruit in training. A woman with purpose and new-found direction.

That first morning in my dorm I changed into my uniform. Easing into a fawn, long-sleeved dress with starched, detachable white collars and cuffs, I fastened a white apron round my waist, tied up the brown Petersham bow at my neck, and completed the outfit with a beautiful wool cloak and felt hat, before standing back to admire the look in a small mirror inside my wardrobe.

As a steady stream of spring sunshine shone through the ever-open window, I smiled at the smart young lady gazing back at me.

A nanny was born!

My mother had never had the chance to pursue her dreams, but now, thanks to her, I could. And do you know, from that moment on I never looked back.

There is little I haven't come up against in the years since I began my training. In my first book, *A Spoonful of Sugar*, I shared many stories about how I graduated straight into the turmoil of the Second World War and how difficult it was caring for children during those trying years.

Bombs, bed-wetting, bullying, absent mothers, sick children, freezing winters, disease, adultery, deserters, scandal, inspiring evacuees and their memorable cockney mothers – they all certainly conspired to make my life interesting and provided some training ground for a new graduate. Thanks to the war and the communities within which I worked my eyes were certainly opened to the ways of the world.

The hostilities also catapulted me headlong into some of the most bewildering, exhausting, frightening and challenging moments of my career, but I, like every sensible British woman I knew, never allowed terror to take hold.

We had no choice but to go about our business, running the home, shopping, cooking and keeping the nation's children happy, healthy and as well fed as rations allowed, while chaos erupted around us. Every fibre of my being remained focused on the welfare of the children in my care. Nothing was more important than being the most loving and professional nanny that I could possibly be.

After graduating in 1940, I cared for frightened evacuees, poverty-stricken East End tough nuts, fragile Jewish refugees and children of all ages, backgrounds and races. The war made chameleons of us all and I quickly realised I had to be adaptable and open-minded to blend in with all backgrounds, classes and personalities, especially if I was to be a truly effective nanny.

The last two years of the war were spent running Redbourn Day Nursery in Hertfordshire, caring for children whose mothers were out working at war factories, doing their bit for the war effort. It was the most eye-opening and rewarding time of my career, and I fervently hoped I treated each and every child at the nursery with the same level of dignity, respect and love they all deserved.

With the end of the war, however, the nursery lost its soul and I my enthusiasm for it. Mothers were slowly trickling back into their homes and children were being withdrawn from the nursery in their droves. My presence there simply wasn't needed any longer and I felt as though I was simply going through the motions. Handing in my notice wasn't a hard decision. I was eager to get into a private household and work one-on-one with a family who needed my help.

But in March 1946, with postwar austerity biting, did I have a place in this strange new world?

The skies were finally clear of enemy bombers and flying rockets, but did danger still lurk in the bomb-scarred streets? Would a nanny in uniform be welcome in a British home?

Only one way to find out.

Switching off the lights and shutting the door of the day nursery behind me for the last time, I strode outside and into an uncertain future.

NANNY'S WISDOM

A house is just a building
A house is just that, four walls made of bricks and filled with material items. It's not the house and the expense of the items in it that count – it's the occupants that really matter. Whether you live in a castle or a shack, you can really only find true and lasting happiness if the house in which you live is filled with family and love. Only then, when a house is ringing with laughter and people you worship, can it become a home. So next time you find yourself wishing you lived in a bigger house with more space and rooms, think again. During my childhood I lived in large houses and tiny bungalows and I had just as many fun times in each. Wealth, riches and a big fancy kitchen don't matter. It's people who count.

Surprise your children
Every now and again why not do what my father did and surprise them with some wonderful sweets in a brown paper bag? Watch their eyes light up when you pull the bag out of your pocket. Not too often, mind you . . .

Encourage children's strengths and not their weaknesses
While I was floundering at school and feeling quite inferior to my big sister Kathleen, my mother, quite rightly, explained that I was just as clever as my sister but that I had different talents and skills. Hers lay in academic pursuits, I was more practical and better with my hands. Don't focus on what your child can't do. Instead find out what he or she is good at or enjoys and encourage that instead.

2

Saints and Sinners

Ride a cock-horse to Banbury Cross,
To see a fine lady upon a white horse;
Rings on her fingers and bells on her toes,
And she shall have music wherever she goes.
Tradional English nursery rhyme

It was a most intriguing request and one I knew I couldn't possibly ignore. 'I really am in the most urgent need of help for my wife,' said the gentleman's voice on the other end of the phone. 'Meet me at Fortnum and Mason in London's Piccadilly and I shall explain more over tea. I will be wearing a bowler hat and carrying a cane. Good day to you, Nurse.'

The Norland had arranged my first interview for private work.

Postwar Britain was a much-changed place. Economy and survival were the order of the day as women and returning soldiers struggled to find their places in the world. But to what world had many of them returned? The answer was uncertain.

There were major shortages of jobs and housing, but people were being looked after in ways never seen or heard of before. The new Labour government brought in the National Insurance Act, which marked the beginning of the welfare state. All working adults paid National Insurance, which was used to pay for free health care, state pensions and an allowance for those forced to take a break from employment.

Mothers received a lump-sum payment on the birth of each child, and if they had been paying National Insurance they also received an allowance for eighteen weeks after the birth. Thanks to the work that I and thousands like me had done in war nurseries, the government began to take a more collective view of childcare and of the state's involvement in families and child-rearing.

In 1945, the Family Allowances Act became law, and at the same time the School Milk Act came into force, ensuring that all schoolchildren would receive a third of a pint of milk each day.

These measures led to a new feeling of determination and the optimistic feeling that come what may, things should be 'better'. Before, bombs and rationing had been at the forefront of everyone's minds; now it was all about putting the family first, and rightly so if you ask me. But while we all looked forward, it was impossible to ignore the past entirely.

The scars of Hitler's terrifying attacks had left behind a sobering legacy. Once glorious buildings had crumbled to dust, blown-out houses lay empty and devoid of life, closed streets and roofless houses could be seen all over the land. Pavements in the cities were pockmarked with bomb craters and 'Keep Out' signs on bombsites acted like magnets to naughty children seeking out thrills.

But there was also optimism amongst the rubble. We had survived. We owed it to those who had sacrificed their lives for our freedom to restore our great cities. Part of winning the war required an acceptance of those sacrifices and a willingness to rebuild our country from the ashes up.

As always, the *Norland Quarterly*, the newsletter the Norland sent out to all its nurses, past and present, put fire in our bellies and made us feel we were never truly alone. Indeed, we were an army of nannies, scattered all over the world but linked by our extraordinary training and our belief in the Norland motto: 'Love Never Faileth'.

Nursery life can at times be a somewhat solitary life, so the exchange of experiences between nurses in the newsletters was so engaging.

'The post-war period has been one of considerable difficulty,' wrote Mrs Blakeney, the new principal of the recently renamed Norland College (it changed its status from institute to college in 1946 to sound more modern).

War was a most trying time. We did not know from term to term where teaching would be taking place. In March 1944 a canister of incendiary bombs was dropped on the Nurseries, with no loss to any personnel but with much damage to property. We had 14 rooms out of action. The fact that there was no loss of life was due to everyone knowing what to do at a given time. Then came the flying-bomb period and we were forced to disperse for three months. I confess to being very thankful when the last rocket dropped. I express my admiration for all our Norland Nurses and their courage, patience and perseverance under such trying circumstances.

I feel the following lines of Matthew Arnold are expressive of your work.

> *Beacons of hope, ye appear!*
> *Langour is not in your heart,*
> *Weakness is not in your word,*
> *Weariness not on your brow.*
> *Ye alight in our van! at your voice,*
> *Panic, despair, flee away.*
> *Ye move through the ranks, recall*
> *The stragglers, refresh the outworn,*
> *Praise, re-inspire the brave!*
> *Order, courage, return.*
> *Eyes rekindling, and prayers,*
> *Follow your steps as ye go.*
> *Ye fill up the gaps in our files,*
> *Strengthen the wavering line,*
> *Stablish, continue our march,*
> *On, to the bound of the waste,*
> *On, to the City of God.*

And so it was that I took a red double-decker bus up Piccadilly in smart Mayfair to continue my own personal march and meet this rather desperate gentleman to answer his call for help.

I too had to look forward not back. With state-run colleges opening up everywhere to train nursery nurses, employing a private nanny in a uniform was not regarded as prestigious as it once had been. No, I should feel most grateful for a position in a house, however difficult it might be.

Liveried doormen graciously swung open the door to Fortnum & Mason for me.

War may have altered England, but some traditions would never die out.

Hitler had dumped 18,000 tonnes of explosives on London, but Fortnum & Mason at 181 Piccadilly had survived. Afternoon tea here was an iconic British symbol and I was pleased to see the place was thronged with customers nibbling dainty sandwiches and sipping tea. Had Hitler really believed that he could replace our beloved cucumber sandwiches with stollen and bratwurst?

Once inside a welcoming rush of warmth hit me. Smartly dressed waitresses rushed about the place carrying tea trays piled high with fresh leaf tea brewing in bone-china teapots and plates of little cucumber sandwiches with the crusts cut off.

It reminded me of a special day when my mother and I had gone for tea at Lyons Corner House as a treat for being accepted by the Norland all those years before. How different a person I was now to back then! But then war had no doubt altered us all.

I caught sight of a lone gentleman with a cane resting against the white linen tablecloth. Dressed smartly in a double-breasted dark suit and cravat, he looked like a well-to-do banker or merchant.

As soon as he saw me, he smiled, took off his bowler hat and rose to his feet. 'Miss Ashford?' he enquired.

'Mr Sacks?' I smiled.

'Yes indeed,' he smiled warmly back, pulling out my chair for me. 'I can't tell you how grateful I am to see you.'

Soon I found my plate piled high with sandwiches and a delicate little cup of the most delicious-smelling tea pressed into my hands. I took a sip and eyed the cakes that our waitress had brought to the table. Delicate little sponges and scones that looked as light as gossamer sat tantalisingly atop a white doily. We'd never had anything as refined as that at my last job at the Redbourn day nursery. I smiled, picturing the face of little Jimmy if someone had ever set down a plate of such delicacies in front of *him*.

Jimmy was quite the most delightful little boy I had ever cared for, and in many ways was responsible for making me a more well-rounded nanny, a nanny without prejudice if you like.

I had met four-year-old Jimmy whilst working at the Redbourn Day Nursery. An evacuee, he was the youngest of twelve children. His mother, one Gladys Trump, was quite the most ferocious woman I had ever come across. Up until then I had mainly cared for the pampered offspring of the well-to-do, parents who thought nothing of entrusting their children to my care in a well-stocked and comfortable nursery. Often the only time they would see their children would be for an hour after tea in the drawing room.

Little Jimmy and his mother had come from a somewhat less comfortable environment. They hailed from the impoverished East End. Instead of a plush townhouse or a country estate, all thirteen of the Trumps were crammed into a two-bedroom flat in Stepney. It's impossible to overstate how poor – not to mention how dirty – little Jimmy and his mother were. I'm ashamed to say I sat in judgement of Gladys, and she and I locked horns on a number of occasions. I took Jimmy's raggedy, dirty clothes and filthy, scrawny body to be signs of neglect and tutted as I stripped him down and bathed him. Gracious, the commotion when Gladys found out her precious son had been bathed! She'd pushed her face so close to mine I could see my face reflected in her eyeballs. 'He ain't 'avin' no barf,' she'd scowled.

I couldn't for the life of me understand why she couldn't bear her son to be bathed and so I continued, even after she sewed little Jimmy into his clothes to stop me! 'This boy shall be bathed daily,' I'd muttered as I grimly unpicked the stitches.

The war between us had raged on until a kindly local midwife opened my eyes to a number of things. She explained that women like Gladys didn't bathe their sons because they genuinely believed they would catch their death of cold, and that the only baths they had were filled with coal.

I'll admit, I hung my head when that midwife explained in graphic detail the abject poverty in which Jimmy and his mother usually lived.

'What you have to understand, Nurse Brenda,' she'd said, 'is that she has raised twelve children more or less single-handedly in a tiny two-bedroom flat in the Peabody Buildings in Stepney. Those buildings are notorious. They are infested with bugs and in all honesty should probably have been bulldozed years ago.

'You cannot imagine the poverty. Picture the scene, Brenda,' she'd urged. 'Thirteen of them in a dirty tenement flat. There are no facilities in those flats. The only water comes from a single tap at the end of each balcony, where the only lavatory is situated. There would be small children everywhere, naked from the waist down to save on washing.'

Humiliation washed over me as I thought back to my own comfortable childhood home. The beautiful detached Surrey house surrounded by rambling roses and fields had been an idyllic playground in which to while away a blissful childhood. I had been born blessed. Jimmy and his mother had not been.

Did that make them less worthy of my respect? On the contrary, that woman deserved a medal. After that I felt my attitude towards Gladys soften. She had kept her family together under the most miserable, not to mention terrifying, circumstances. She loved the bones off her children, and that was to be admired, not sneered at.

Meeting little Jimmy had taught me an important lesson: never judge until one knows the full story. That said, I never did get him entirely clean, despite my best efforts with a scrubbing brush, but by the time he left me he was quite the most delightful child you could ever hope to set eyes on. Bright, enquiring, mischievous, with eyes as green as an alpine meadow.

I could picture them now, twinkling with glee and as large as gobstoppers if he were ever to set eyes on such a delicious afternoon tea! I dare say it would have been demolished in the blink of an eye.

Rationing was still in full swing despite the end of the war, indeed bread was more tightly rationed in 1946 than it was during the war as the economy attempted to recover. It could still be bought, however, if you had the money to pay for it, which, judging by his smart appearance and the leather briefcase by his chair, Mr Sacks obviously did. We may have only been a few miles from the bomb-shattered East End, but the world that Mr Sacks inhabited was obviously a million miles from young Jimmy's.

Fortunately, the Norland was still supporting the East End children all it could with its Norland Nurses mission fund. Before war broke out it had supported the Bethnal Green Day Nurseries, but they had now been disbanded and I had been reading of our efforts to help St Paul's Day Nursery in the badly bombed London docks. One Norland Nurse had written about her recent visit in the *Norland Quarterly*.

The Nursery was started over 60 years ago, in fields which today are dockyards, stores and filthy streets. The inhabitants are of all colours and nationalities.

Passing through a bombed alley, it is pleasant to come upon a square of peace and greenness, where the nursery is. Myself and a friend had been worried for some time at the lack of education at this nursery so we offered our services for a month. There was slight resentment from the staff to begin with, coming in, and as they thought, creating havoc. This did not last long however.

We started the day with singing and games and then encouraged the children to paint. All the children loved this and all wanted to paint aeroplanes. Sand has been the greatest thrill of all and with lots of water has provided unending joy. We had a glorious flood in the garden the first day from all the sand and water! We got the sand by bravely going into the Funeral Furnishing and Monuments storehouse. They did not sell sand, but were most kind in giving us three sackfuls. We also managed to make a Wendy house, with an old clothes horse and a deckchair frame. We were asked continually 'Can we do this again tomorrow? When are you coming again?' The children are more alert and coordinated already. Come and visit the nursery and please give your money – it is desperately needed – because it is a positive way of showing that Norland want an equal chance of happiness for every child.

Upon reading of the efforts of two such inspirational and resourceful nurses I had made a mental note to visit. Who knew? I might even see little Jimmy there.

Now, however, my attention had to be focused not on the East End children, or the mouthwatering tea in front of me, but upon Mr Sacks and his apparent emergency.

'Do tell me about your situation and then I can see whether I can be of assistance,' I said, smiling.

'My wife Carolyn has four children, two boys aged two and a half and four and a half and baby twins, one boy and one girl, born just a few weeks ago.'

'Gracious,' I said. 'You do have a houseful.'

'Quite honestly, I don't know how she's coping,' he said. 'She is exhausted. '

Suddenly I realised he too had dark circles under his eyes. 'Oh you poor thing,' I gushed.

He sighed as he took a bite out of his cucumber sandwich and chewed thoughtfully.

'On top of which poor Carolyn's father is gravely ill and on his deathbed, so we need to move in with him.'

His voice dropped to a whisper and he glanced left and right. I leaned in closer.

'We rather suspect his carer is manipulating him. He has altered his will and left everything to her,' he muttered. 'So the move is of the utmost urgency, as I'm sure you can appreciate.'

My eyes grew as wide as saucers. 'Oh absolutely I understand,' I said, nodding vigorously.

That poor, desperate couple. Baby twins, two toddlers, a house move, a dying relative and a fraudster to contend with. If ever a family were in dire need of help it was surely them! I decided to take the job before he had even offered it to me.

'We'll need you right away, Nurse Ashford. You will take the job, won't you?'

No sooner had I nodded than he stood up and put on his bowler hat with a flourish and beamed brightly.

'Marvellous. The salary will be £15 a week and you can report to my wife tomorrow.'

With that he strode from Fortnum & Mason, hailed a cab and vanished into the bustle of Piccadilly.

I sat back in my chair, my head still spinning from the speed of my new appointment. Fifteen pounds a week? It wasn't much, the same or even less than I'd been earning in my previous jobs, but even if he'd given me the chance I doubted I'd have argued with him over it. I'm not very money-motivated, you see. Just as well, as you don't go into childcare for money; you do it for love.

It was only later, when I packed my suitcase and uniform ready for my new job, that I realised. He hadn't paid for our tea! Little did I know it then, but I was about to become embroiled in a most peculiar world.

On the way to my new job I made a mental note to tell my new friend of this startling event to see what he would make of it.

At the mere thought of dear sweet Bill I felt a warm glow spread through me. Former Spitfire pilot Bill was quite, quite lovely, delicious in fact, and the reason that I'd been wearing a smile like summer these past few months.

With his blond hair, big brown eyes and earnest countenance, Bill was very much up my street. We'd met recently at a religious rally in Hildenborough in Kent. Religious camps or rallies, as they were known, were springing up all over Britain. They were extremely popular in the postwar years and offered direction to thousands of youths. For young men and women who had survived countless brushes with death and seen their homes bombed and their loved ones killed, these conferences offered hope in uncertain times.

I'd gone hoping to finding peace and I'd met Bill. We were introduced by my friend Mary, who'd been wide-eyed as she'd told me about him on the train there.

'You'll like Bill, he's lovely,' she'd gushed. 'Very bright. He's studying theology at Cambridge University. Fearfully clever.'

It turned out that Bill had flown Spitfires in the RAF during the war.

'Terribly brave,' Mary had continued, her voice dropping a decibel or two. 'Do you know, when he was out on a secret sortie somewhere over Europe in his Spitfire he experienced something that made him convert and decide to give his life to the Lord.'

'Gosh,' I'd gulped, my eyes growing wide. 'Converted in the skies. I wonder what happened to have given him such a profound moment?'

I never did find out what happened that day in the Spitfire, but whatever it was, his love for the Lord was now beyond question. He loved Christ almost as much as · I loved babies, and that really was saying something!

One evening I'd watched him out the corner of my eye during a prayer meeting. His eyes had been closed and a look of utter peace washed over his face as he'd silently mouthed the prayers. I'd marvelled at the strength of his faith and bathed in the gentle aura of serene reverence that surrounded him.

He was nothing like my first boyfriend, a cocky, boastful young man by the name of Henry who'd done the dirty on me with another woman. I had really hoped that Henry might be the man for me, that we could settle down and have babies together. But those dreams had been shattered in a heartbeat when I discovered he'd been stringing me and another woman along at the same time.

When the other woman, whom he'd been engaged to, had got wind of our relationship she'd threatened to sue him for breach of promise. Henry's promise to marry this lady could have been considered a legally binding contract and he'd obviously taken her threats to sue him seriously. Perhaps she had already given up her virginity to him and, horrified to find out about me, had been concerned with the damage to her reputation and the loss of status. Changing morals have all but led to the collapse of this kind of action, but back in 1942 breach of promise was taken seriously.

I sincerely doubted, though, that Bill was a man who would indulge in such dangerous, dark behaviour. He was a war hero, after all, a man at peace with himself and the world. A man I had well and truly fallen for.

Back then I was as naive and innocent as they came, but even so, I knew that many people had had affairs left, right and centre during the war and illegitimate babies were commonplace. Desperate women had sought comfort whenever or wherever they could. Adultery had been rife. The brief encounter became a common experience as servicemen and women and civilians sought comfort where they could find it. I suppose every day you are alive in such conditions is a gift and made people behave in ways they would never normally. I even cared for the child of one woman who had *five* more children with another man whilst her husband was away fighting. Amazingly, when her husband returned from the war he not only forgave her, but helped to raise the illegitimate children. What a saint!

I didn't stand in judgement, just looked on with a sort of bewildered dismay. My sheltered childhood hadn't left me prepared for such behaviour. We never learned about the birds and bees at school and my mother never taught me anything. I had a vague sense that babies came about as the result of some sort of physical intimacy, and I knew that such a thing was meant to happen only within marriage – I had, after all, met plenty of illegitimate babies and their poor mothers. But I was stunningly innocent and as a twenty-five-year-old embarking on my second relationship I was as naive as they came.

Bill had invited me to visit him at university in Cambridge. I couldn't wait and on my next weekend off I intended to take him up on his offer.

Arriving at my new employers, I forced all thoughts of romance from my head as I knocked on the door of a very ordinary semi in Pinner, Greater London.

Mr Sacks, still immaculately turned out in his pinstripe suit, answered the door with a charming smile.

'Ah, the cavalry has arrived. Welcome, Nurse Brenda. Come in, come in, do.'

I had already resolved on the way there not to make mention of the small matter of the unpaid tea bill and to put it down to a bad memory on his part.

He led me along a small corridor and into the sitting room.

'This is my wife Carolyn,' he said.

There, huddled on the sofa, was the most pitiful sight I'd seen since little Jimmy had been brought into the day nursery.

Carolyn was tall, pale, thin and looked utterly worn out. Clutched to each breast were two red and wriggly little babies who were incandescent with rage and hunger.

My heart went out to this poor exhausted woman.

'I can't seem to feed them,' she sobbed in despair over their angry cries.

Straight away I realised what the problem was. I'd seen it during my training when caring for a young girl and her illegitimate baby. Her milk hadn't come in. The more an exhausted mother frets and worries, the less likely her milk is to come in, the hungrier the baby gets and the more worried the mother becomes. A vicious circle if ever I saw one. It was my job to ease her load.

'Come here,' I soothed. 'Will you allow me to hold one?'

With dull and unsmiling eyes, she handed me one of her babies.

Violet and Peter were beautiful little babies with masses of dark curly hair, but I could see Carolyn was too tired to appreciate the little miracles she had produced.

'Glad you ladies are sorted then,' piped up Mr Sacks from the corner of the room. 'I'll be off out then.' Bang, the door shut after him and he was off, whistling up the street and swinging his brolly without a care in the world.

I turned back to his poor scrap of a wife. I'd never seen anyone so thin after giving birth.

'Tell you what,' I said softly. 'How's about I make you a milky drink?'

Propping her up against freshly plumped cushions, I sorted out her two older boys with some toys, then went to the kitchen and fixed her a nice milky drink, a cheese and pickle sandwich and two chocolate biscuits.

'Chocolate's just the thing for helping to produce rich breast milk,' I winked.

When she had eaten and was more comfortable and rested, I showed her how to do breast massage.

'Don't worry,' I smiled reassuringly. 'We'll get your babies feeding in no time.'

Sure enough, with plenty of rest, fresh air and regular

food, within days the colour had come back into her cheeks, her breasts were engorged with milk and the babies were feeding happily.

She and I took it in turns to hold Violet and Peter, so that she didn't need to feed them both at the same time. I also showed her the correct way to position the baby and how to ensure they latched on properly and got a good flow of mother's milk. Next, we sorted out a regular feeding and sleeping pattern that I kept note of and made sure we stuck to. I kept her older boys entertained too, so that she and her twins got regular naps.

Violet and Peter began to thrive, her boys looked less surly and Carolyn looked so grateful. Peace was restored in Pinner.

'Thank you so much, Nurse Brenda,' she smiled one night over the boys' teatime. 'You're a miracle worker.'

'I don't know about that,' I chuckled. 'It's simple really. All babies thrive on routine – that and love.'

I hadn't been there long when the big move to Grandpa's house in Kent was announced.

'We can't possibly move with the babies,' fretted Carolyn, her lip wobbling. 'How will I pack and get everything sorted with them?'

'Don't worry,' I soothed. 'I'll take the babies off for the day. I know someone who would simply love to meet them.'

Leaving the rest of the family amongst a mountain of packing boxes, I headed to Mother and Father's house in St Albans with the twins.

Mother was still bereft after losing her beloved little Sally, an evacuee whom she had cared for throughout the

Second World War and whose own mother now wanted her home with her.

Everyone felt for the parents of evacuees, and rightly so. One can only imagine the anguish of waving off your bewildered son or daughter at a train station teeming with other heartbroken parents and scared little children, all in the knowledge that you didn't know when you might hold him or her in your arms again.

But what of the 'other parents'? The thousands of women like my mother who cared so devotedly for other women's children throughout the terrifying war years? All over England bonds were formed, motherly love blossomed and 'surrogate' mothers were born. I knew better than anyone how much you can grow to love a child that hasn't sprung from your own loins and I doubted Mother was alone. There must have been countless other women who were feeling the aching loss of an evacuee they'd cared for and would probably never see again.

Mother never said as much as she wasn't the type to complain, but I knew she was feeling the loss of Sally. Seeing these gorgeous little bundles would cheer her up no end.

When she answered the door I could see she'd been baking: she was wiping her hands on a white apron and the faintest trace of flour dusted her soft downy face. Her eyes went from me to the twins all propped up in their big coach pram under a snowy white blanket. I had to admit, with their soft dark curls and cupid-bow mouths they did look simply adorable.

Mother's hands flew to her face. 'Oh Brenda,' she

gasped. 'Aren't they beautiful. Come in, come in, you'll catch your death of cold. I've just baked some jam tarts.'

As she bustled into the warm kitchen and put the kettle on the stove, I marvelled at Mother's ability to make every house a home. Within ten minutes I was nursing a hot cup of tea and Mother was cradling one twin in each arm. She radiated happiness.

'I've got a marvellous idea,' she said. 'Why don't we take them to a photographer's and have some photos taken?'

Her eyes shone with so much excitement I had to laugh. 'How can I say no?'

Mother proudly pushed the twins along the street in their pram, showing them off to friends and neighbours on the way. 'Brenda's new charges,' she explained.

Bless her. She would so have loved to have had twins. When I was growing up, Kathleen and I had constantly found ourselves dressed alike!

The war in some senses had been so good for Mother – she had had evacuees coming out of her ears and plenty of little folk to care for. But now, with the war over, the evacuees had returned to their parents, Father was working hard in London and my four brothers were either at school or at work. I suspected that beneath the bright smiles loneliness lingered.

Women like my mother were born to care and nurture; it was virtually imprinted in her DNA. To find her home empty of children for the first time in twenty-five years must have come as a dreadful shock.

Kathleen was working long, long hours as a midwife,

though, like me, she visited when she could. Thanks to the war, my siblings and I were essentially strangers. We'd tried to keep up with snail-mail letters, but we'd barely seen each other these past five years, so busy were we all off doing our own things.

With the war now over, I was looking forward to getting to know Kathleen again, but 1946 marked the start of the baby boom. Prewar relationships were resumed and birth rates went through the roof. Seeing as Kathleen was a midwife and I a nanny, it rather looked like that relationship might have to wait a little longer to be renewed.

For my mother, like so many others who had no job to fall back on, readjusting was a struggle.

'Are you OK, Mother?' I asked as we walked to the photographer's.

'I'm fine, darling,' she smiled, pausing briefly to tuck a stray hair behind my ear. I had to laugh. I was still her little girl, even after all these years. 'Don't you worry about me,' she added.

We had a whale of a time that afternoon, dressing up the babies in pretty bonnets and having their photos taken, followed by tea and a stroll in the park. By the time Mother and I returned home I could see she was brimming over with stories to tell Father when he returned after work.

'Thank you, Brenda,' she said as Mr Sacks' car arrived to take us to our new residence. 'That was a tonic.'

Seeing Mother was a tonic to me, too, and I felt fully restored. I was twenty-five, but with the war and running Redbourn Day Nursery I felt years older. Yet despite all that I had seen and experienced, I didn't feel too old to still need my mother's love and bathe in the warmth of her company. She made having a family seem the easiest and most natural thing in the world.

Having children and a family to call my own hadn't happened to me yet, and I'll admit there was a part of me that longed to know the love a mother feels cradling her baby. I lived in hope that my time would come and I would have the honour of making my mother a grand-mother. Remembering Bill, a soft flush rose up my chest and I smiled a secret little smile as I clambered into the car.

'Bye, Mother,' I grinned, waving furiously as the car pulled off up the street.

Pulling up outside Carolyn's father's house, I could see our new home was somewhat grander than the old semi. The large detached house was set in its own grounds and was surrounded by beautiful blue rhodo-dendron bushes. A garage annexe contained a little studio flat above it.

Inside, the boys chased each other happily through the packing boxes that were strewn over the large hallway as Carolyn busily unpacked.

'Hush, boys,' she called. 'You'll wake Grandpa.' She turned to me. 'He is bedbound,' she explained. 'There's a new male carer – Charlie got rid of the last one – so you won't have much to do with Grandpa.'

Grandpa had good taste. The sideboards were groaning with lovely ornaments. A rich mahogany display cabinet glittered with silver and an exquisite duck-egg-blue china tea set. Beautiful oil paintings hung from a picture rail. I sighed. I should never have the money to buy such things.

Little matter. Money wasn't the most important thing. Even so . . .

'Mr Sacks,' I called brightly as he walked past carrying a box of china to the garage. 'It's my day off and I don't seem to have been paid yet.'

He paused and a muscle under his eye twitched.

'Yes, yes, of course, Nurse Ashford,' he blustered. 'Terribly sorry, I just forgot. I'll get it tomorrow when I go to London.'

I frowned. This wasn't the first time Mr Sacks had been struck with a bad case of amnesia. The sight of a bill seemed to have an unusual effect on his memory. I'd lost count of the number of times he'd forgotten to pay me my £15 a week.

In fact, pinning down the elusive Mr Sacks was proving increasingly difficult. His hours were so sporadic. Sometimes he would be there all day, at other times he would be gone for hours, not returning until late at night. I never presumed to ask him what he did for a job, one simply didn't with one's employers, but whatever he did for a living, it required a certain degree of ducking and diving.

It was most irksome to have to chase him, but I put it to the back of my mind. Tomorrow was my day off. I was visiting Bill in Cambridge and I was fizzing over with excitement. Carolyn was coping quite nicely now with the twins and was far more settled, so I felt comfortable taking a much-needed day away from my duties.

Bill met me at the station in Cambridge and he was every bit as gentle, kind and sincere as I remembered.

'Let me show you round this beautiful place,' he said, smiling.

I could barely take my eyes off his face. He wasn't brilliantly handsome, but he radiated a goodness that was quite spellbinding.

From there we wandered around. I was totally absorbed in the sights and smells, the dreamy River Cam and its punters, the awe-inspiring King's College Chapel. A place steeped in such history, learning and beauty. I was overawed.

Bill fitted in perfectly. His soft brown eyes shone and he spoke with such passion and conviction as he talked of his studies and what Jesus meant to him.

He encouraged me to talk about my faith and listened, really listened, to what I had to say. He was nothing like cocky, arrogant Henry, my former boyfriend. In fact, he suited me down to the ground.

I found myself wondering yet again what this brave man had witnessed in the dark skies on that sortie in the Spitfire. About what unimaginable horror and fear must have flooded through him as he fought for his life against the Luftwaffe. How had the Lord presented himself to convert Bill there and then in the skies?

Whatever had happened, Bill's faith was as solid as the foundations beneath those grand colleges. His love for the Lord shone from him with an inner radiance.

'He is always there guiding us, Brenda,' he whispered. 'You just have to listen and open your heart. You should come and pray with me soon.'

Staring into those shy and dreamy eyes, I'd have gone to the ends of the earth if he'd asked me. 'I'd like that,' I smiled, flushing pink as candyfloss.

When we parted I longed for him to kiss me, but he simply smiled, shook my hand gently and we made promises to meet again.

On the train, I tingled all over and stroked my hand where he had brushed it. I wanted to hold on to the memory of his touch for as long as possible.

I enjoyed his company. Really enjoyed it. Who knew what the future held?

When I returned home later that evening with a secret smile still playing on my lips, I discovered that we had a new resident in the house. Sitting in the front room with his feet up on the coffee table like he owned the place was a most shifty-looking young man.

'This is Bob,' smiled Carolyn nervously. 'He's a friend of my husband's. He will be staying with us for a while. He's started a business selling toys and he'll be living and working in the studio above the garage.'

Bob was small and twitchy, like a rat, with narrow eyes that darted this way and that. I didn't like the way he was staring at me. The velvet collar of his jacket was turned up and he wore a cocked fedora hat.

What a most peculiar creature.

'Pleased to meet you, Bob,' I said stiffly. 'What an interesting line of work. What sort of toys will you be making?'

'Not sure yet,' he sniffed. 'Play ones, I expect.'

'Right,' I replied, puzzled.

'Anyway,' he said, draining his tea and straightening his kipper tie. 'Just wanted to wet me whistle. I'll be orf now.'

'What time will you be back?' Carolyn enquired.

'See me when you see me,' he called, picking up a small suitcase by his side and heading out the door.

Carolyn turned to me and rolled her eyes.

'Between you and me, I don't much like him,' she confided. 'He never gives a straight answer. He's a bit of a spiv.'

'Hmm,' I murmured. 'I can see.'

'But Charlie says he's down on his luck and needs a hand until he's back on his feet.'

Needed more than a hand to get him back on his feet if you asked me, but I kept my opinion to myself. I was just the nanny after all.

That night I tossed and turned in bed. I thought of Bill, who had made so many sacrifices for his country in the cockpit of his Spitfire. Now this dreadful war was over he was trying to make the best of his situation, following his heart and calling to Jesus. I daresay he had a little money, but this was the age of austerity and he was knuckling down and getting on with it like the best of us. And then there were men like Bob, no doubt pulling scams and dabbling in the black market. Ducking and diving and living above garages. What a strange existence.

This was turning into a very odd place to work indeed! And it was about to get stranger.

Soon after shifty Bob's introduction, an even more peculiar character arrived.

Carolyn had warned me about her brother. 'He's a musician,' she'd said. 'A . . . well . . . how can I say, a colourful character. He does rather tend to turn up when he pleases. You know what musicians are like, they don't keep the same hours as us.'

49

Soon after, I was in the twins' nursery dusting. Grandpa was asleep next door and Mr and Mrs Sacks were out.

'All wight, darlin',' boomed a loud voice up the corridor.

Jumping in shock, I managed to upend my polish and drop my duster. I whirled round and gasped.

Standing before me was a vision in polyester. This must be Trevor the musician.

He was a tiny man, as slight as a sparrow and just as twitchy. His thick dark hair had been slicked back with pomade. A tight, lurid yellow shirt was open nearly to his tummy revealing a thick bush of chest hair. Nestling in that bushy forest twinkled an enormous gold medallion. In fact, everywhere one looked gold seemed to twinkle. Quite extraordinary! Even his fingers were dripping with gold rings.

'Trevor's the name and music's me game,' he chirped. 'And what's your name, darlin'?'

I bristled. I most certainly was not his darling.

'I am Nurse Ashford, the children's nanny,' I replied.

'Course you are, darlin',' he beamed. 'What's a fella got to do to get a cuppa round these parts?' he said, putting his hands on his thrusting hips. 'Me tongue's hanging out.'

He was like nothing I'd ever come across before. I supposed he was embracing the modern trends one kept hearing about. Rock 'n' roll hadn't been invented at that stage, but the music being played was the forerunner to it.

It turned out that Trevor played bebop jazz and boogie-woogie blues on his piano in pubs.

'You should come and see me play tonight?' he grinned, heading to the kitchen.

'I can't,' I said. 'I'm working.' In any case I couldn't bear the smell of beer and never set foot in pubs.

In the coming months, Trevor turned up sporadically and never with any warning. I began to feel as though I was living in a comedy of errors. He would sneak up behind me and frighten the life out of me with a booming 'All wight darlin'?' His outfits grew more outrageous with the passing months. No combination of clothing was off limits. From dayglo shirts teamed with bright patterned trousers to cocked fedora hats and loud kipper ties, Trevor could always be relied on to add a garish splash of colour to the house.

What Miss Whitehead, my former principal and a stickler for a properly turned-out uniform, would have made of this flash Harry, goodness only knows.

Between alarming Trevor and shifty Bob, who lurked in the shadows and scared me half to death, I was a bag of nerves.

What effect all these comings and goings were having on the children was anybody's business. It was most disconcerting. On the whole, though, thanks to separate day and night nurseries, the children didn't seem too put out by the mayhem created by these bizarre characters.

Children by and large are fairly resilient and not easy to shock. The boys took these shifty men in their stride. As ever in 1940s households, the Sacks children were confined to certain areas of the house, such as the day and night nurseries, kitchen and garden. They would no more play on their hands and knees with their trains in the living room than I would. This meant, luckily, that they mainly saw their mother, father and me.

With four children under five, I had to run that household with a meticulous eye for detail and a consistent routine. Whilst the elder children were playing with their toys and the twins were napping, I would lay out their clothes for the next day, wash bottles or catch up with any of the countless tasks that seemed to make up my day. I was forever looking ahead (not to mention left and right) to see what tasks I could complete to save time and confusion in my day. Carolyn cooked, so I didn't have to make their meals, but keeping all four entertained, fed, watered and happily playing was most certainly a full-time job that involved a high degree of stamina.

I couldn't take my eye off the ball for a moment, and if I did you could be sure chaos would break out. One afternoon I was trying to change the twins' nappies when I heard the most terrific din downstairs.

Trevor was doing a full-throttle rendition of a jazz number on the piano in the room below. It sounded like a stray cat being strangled.

'Really,' I muttered, securing Violet's terry-cloth nappy with a large safety pin. 'This is quite intolerable.'

'Don't leave the room, boys,' I ordered the older two, and having made sure the twins were safely in their cots I stormed downstairs and told Trevor, in no uncertain terms, that his playing was more than my ears could tolerate.

Dodging Bob on the landing – he was just going out, or was he returning? one never knew – I let myself back into the nursery, shut the door and fell back against it with a big sigh.

My relief was short-lived.

'What on earth?' I gasped.

The boys had somehow managed to get hold of a pot of Trevor's pomade and had smeared it all over their hair and faces. They had also tried on every piece of clothing they owned. Pullovers were bundled over shirts and they had socks on their hands!

The twins were an eager audience to this hectic scene and were sitting up in their cots giggling and banging the cot bars with the pomade lid.

'We're putting on a show for the twins, Nanny,' piped up the older boy.

By the time I had cleared up the mess I was quite exhausted. Thank goodness poor old Grandpa was bedbound. It was far and away the safest place for him to be!

With days such as these, there was scarcely an evening when my head did not hit the pillow and I was sound asleep by 10 p.m. Even if I had wanted to watch thrusting Trevor showing off on his piano down the pub, I would never have had the energy to stay awake.

And throughout all this bedlam, Mr Sacks still kept conveniently forgetting to pay me my wages.

One morning, about five months after I started, I had had enough. He was late paying me again and yet only the day before I'd seen him counting a big wad of money.

'I shall need paying promptly each week,' I said sharply.

'Nurse Ashford,' he said smoothly. 'Don't fret. I won't see you short.'

That evening he arrived home late, having been in London with the eldest boy.

'Where did you go today?' I asked the boy as I was helping him into his pyjamas. 'Anywhere nice?'

'I played the piano at Harrods,' he answered.

'Oh,' I said. 'Were you trying one out to buy?'

'Oh no,' he replied. 'Dad and I just go all over.'

Suddenly I began to see clearly for the first time. The image of the professional City gent that Mr Sacks had presented to me all those months ago in Fortnum & Mason was totally at odds with reality.

I very much doubted whether the slippery Mr Sacks worked at all. They'd probably only moved into this house for somewhere bigger to live – nothing to do with a fraudster care assistant.

More likely than not he was gambling, which would explain his erratic hours and why sometimes he had money and other times not. I resolved to say nothing. It wasn't my place to question my boss and I had grown fond of Carolyn and the twins, but a sense of mistrust had settled in my heart towards Mr Sacks and his dubious associates.

The term spiv, used to describe men who ducked and dived, selling things on the black market, was coined in the years immediately after the Second World War. Financially they were lean years, rationing was still biting hard and no one had much money, but still . . . This was my first encounter with people who used the truth sparingly and it wasn't leaving a pleasant taste in my mouth. I adored my charges, but their father left a lot to be desired.

Even I was surprised at what he did next, though. One spring morning, Grandpa died. It had been on the cards. The poor old man couldn't even get out of bed. Carolyn, of course, was distraught and I vowed to help her as much as I could and to take the burden off her shoulders.

I was just taking the twins out one morning when I saw Mr Sacks acting suspiciously by the door, packing things into boxes.

When we returned from our walk, I paused in the hallway. Something was different. Then I realised. The duck-egg china tea set was gone, as were most of the paintings. A faint line of dust outlined where they used to hang on the wall. In fact, anything of value was missing.

'It's all right,' said Carolyn, walking in and seeing my concern. 'Charlie has stored them in next door's cellar to avoid probate.'

Life could be so puzzling. Mother and Father had brought me up to tell the absolute truth at all times. Behaving in this deceitful way was against everything I held dear. Bill would never have dreamed of behaving in such a way.

The only upside was that Bob hadn't been seen around lately and had seemingly vanished off the face of the earth. I'll admit it, I felt relieved now that he wasn't sidling around the place like a shifty hyena.

Around the same time I received a phone call that saddened me to the core. It was my friend Mary, whom I'd had to thank for meeting Bill. Nothing had happened between Bill and me yet, but I had so enjoyed that wonderful day in Cambridge and I couldn't wait to plan another visit.

'Did you know Bill has decided to become celibate?' she asked.

She paused and her words hung in the air.

I felt my heart sink like a stone in water.

'Celibate?' I choked finally. 'N . . . no,' I stuttered. 'No, I didn't know that.'

'Yes,' she went on. 'Apparently he has decided to give himself to the Lord completely.'

She carried on talking, but I had stopped listening. I found I had a sudden lump in my throat.

Despair engulfed me. I had thought so fondly of Bill, had even half hoped I might fit into his future plans somewhere. He had touched my heart and left a permanent mark.

I placed a hand on my chest and breathed out slowly.

How could he be celibate? How?

My legs wobbled just a little and I sat down heavily on a hall chair. I couldn't blame Bill, he was following his heart just as I had always done, and now it seemed only one person featured in his life – not me, but Jesus! First Henry and his betrayal and now this?

I suppose in many ways it would have been so easy to up sticks and escape, to get a job working abroad for a wealthy family, as so many of my contemporaries were doing in the late 1940s and early 1950s. One had only to read of their exploits in the *Norland Quarterly* to feel that strong tug of wanderlust.

'I am serving with the wife of the British ambassador in Washington but had cause, along with two other Norlanders working in Washington, to visit New York for a Norland reunion,' wrote one Nurse Armitage.

We travelled the 300 miles or so on a super new train, the last word in luxury, almost out of this world. At intervals a coloured man walks down the aisle with a large basket full of sandwiches, milk, candy bars, cookies, etc. One could become very lazy in America, as everything is done for one.

Upon arriving New York is one seething mass of people. I cannot describe the splendour of the store windows. It's like looking into fairyland. There is Santa Claus and characters out of Walt Disney films all moving about. They appear to be dancing and singing, and the recorded music plays all day and comes through loud speakers in the windows. It is quite a sight for the children.

Flats in America are called apartments. We had a buffet supper in a lovely room with a huge window the entire length of the room. It was a wonderful sight up on the twelfth floor, looking at New York lighted up by night.

New York sounded quite the place to be. But not as impressive as an account of travel in Kenya by the patriotically named Kathleen England.

I travelled by sea to Kenya. We are twelve miles from Nanyuki, our nearest township, we have no telephone, only wireless. The house is all made of wood and I have a nursery wing attached to the house. The gardens are lovely with all kinds of flowers in bloom throughout the year. Mount Kenya is at the back of the house, with snow on its summit, and it looks wonderful shrouded in cloud, with just the peak towering above.

After the rationing and scarcity of domestic labour in England, it's marvellous to be able to sit down to a meal ready prepared, with abundant supplies of butter and cream. It always surprises me how good the native servant can be in the house and how well he can cook, at it is so different to his mode of life.

But if one were to feel jealous of Nurse England's abundant supplies whilst rationing was still firmly in place at home, one only had to read Nurse Nina Baker's account of her time in Marrakesh to feel blessed again.

The medina in Marrakesh is enormous, and consists of all these narrow passages, which are then divided into sections, pottery, shoes, spices, etc. The whole area smells very unpleasant, as the Arabs have no idea of sanitation and there are a great deal of laden donkeys, mules and hundreds of people jostling to and fro. Occasionally one meets a row of beggars in a miserable state, many with sickly infants, hired or bought for the purpose of collecting alms. The alleys have large doors at intervals, which are closed when some evil-doer is trying to escape, perhaps one who has stolen from a store or knifed an enemy.

The most interesting part is the Market Square. The morning is spent by the Arabs selling their goods, and then there is the barber performing on his clients, not to mention the dentist, appeasing the agonies of his, with considerable pressure, and the waterman, intermingling with the crowd, with his animal skin full of foul water with which he relieves the thirst of his customers who answer his clanging bell and drink from his shining brass cup. There are snake charmers, flame-eaters, storytellers, acrobats and dancers.

We see the Arabs in the street praying for rain. When there is a rain shortage we get our electricity and water supply cut for two whole days a week. It is then that our thoughts return to England and we realise how fortunate we are in comparison, but the natives think nothing of these shortages, as the women fetch their water from wells in large pots, which they carry gracefully on their heads. They eat very little, and chiefly home-made bread. Their clothes are often very colourful and the women's faces are covered entirely. Their babies are slung across their backs, and they continue their work in spite of their burdens, and the babies are not in the least bit perturbed.

This was a world that I, and the rest of war-weary Britain, had never even imagined existed. Now that the fighting was over and the world was opening up for travel once again, we were finally getting to hear of it. Norlanders were spread far and wide, even in places called Zanzibar.

'This place is delightful,' wrote Nurse Isabelle Atkins.

The island produces coffee, cloves, rice, bananas, coconuts, tangerines, oranges, in fact anything would grow. The Sultan's seventieth birthday was being celebrated and we watched magnificent fireworks before the Royal Palace; we also bathed in Persian baths in a coconut grove. It was here that we saw a very lovely sight, which only happens once in a lifetime – Venus in the centre of a three-day-old moon. I also travelled with my employers to a place called Penang, apparently the real Far East. The harbour was full of all sorts, shapes, sizes and colours of ships and sails. The red and brown sails on Dhows and the gaily painted row boats, with fish's eyes for luck, in which men stand up to row, dressed in many-coloured long skirts, make the whole thing very gay.

Gracious, I'd thought when reading this. It certainly sounded a long way from drizzly England.

But no one's adventures sounded as dramatic as those of Nurse Mary Stephens, who had to journey with her two charges through the Belgian Congo.

We came through the Belgian Congo Customs, where they had shot an elephant the previous night. The tusks were on the lawn outside the hut and many native boys were cutting out pieces of flesh from the huge legs. There were two elephants doing so much damage around the Custom House. They had broken down eighteen banana trees. The native office boy shot the male, and the female elephant charged him but he managed to get away. The amazing thing was that the female elephant tried to lift the dead male elephant with her tusks to get him to shelter.

We passed through a national park and along a glorious river where we saw more elephants drinking. We passed under the Mountains of the Moon, up in the clouds and covered with snow. At night it was too hot to sleep and the sound of frogs was deafening.

We crossed the Semliki River, which was full of crocodiles, on a huge plank laid over three canoes, and the natives used poles to push us over. After that we journeyed into the Eturi Forest, the largest in the world. We saw revolting pygmies, disgusting, shrivelled, animal-looking objects, but gradually intermarrying and getting bigger. The following day we travelled to a game reserve. Here we lived in mud huts, like natives, all inside a compound with the Belgian flag flown high, and six soldiers on duty. We all ate in the hut, where the fattest Belgian woman I have ever seen did the cooking.

My fellow Norlanders' wry look at life abroad amused me no end.

'I think you will be interested to hear from one who has been living in the land of wooden shoes, bulbs and cheese,' wrote Nurse Phyllis Stobbs of her work in Holland in the late 1940s.

Amsterdam is a big bustling city and the traffic moves at a terrific pace. There are a great quantity of bicycles, [and] crossing streets is a hazardous undertaking.

The customs and tastes of the country appeared to have returned to normal and the hardships of war are little mentioned, though deeply felt. Only meat and coffee [are] rationed. There is a pressing need for homes in Holland, there are often two, sometimes three families living in a moderately sized house. The children are plump and bonny, but not as rosy-cheeked as ours.

When in a new country, there is always this tendency to make comparisons. It was carried to extremes by the elderly, prosperous American man who sat behind me on a bus tour. His companion was a keen, enthusiastic Dutch youth, who greatly added to our pleasure with his intelligent comments on the countryside through which we passed. The American seemed unimpressed, and no remark ever came forth other than to make comparisons with the bigger and better ones they had 'back home'.

Nurse Nancy Rowe was relishing her new job in Bermuda after working for four years in a day nursery, just like I had during the war.

'Coming from war-weary England this is paradise,' she wrote. 'Its green-turquoise water, its white limestone houses and its pinky coral beaches, sprinkled with tropical flowers, and its surfeit of good food certainly make one realise that "one half of the world does not realise how the other half lives".'

That might be so, and there was no doubting that all these ladies were clearly having rich experiences, but I agreed with Nurse Edith Merricks, who wrote in the *Norland Quarterly* of her job in South Africa.

The Indian Ocean lies at the bottom of our garden, monkeys run wild and beautiful bunches of bananas grow conveniently near. The bathing is lovely, always surf-riding to be had, as the breakers roll continuously up on to the beach. The white children are very healthy and the native men in the gold mines are very well looked after, with excellent attention in every way.

I see very few prams here in South Africa. All the natives carry their babies tied on their backs and Mammie invariably has a large bundle or a bucket full of water on her head. I am very tempted to stay out in South Africa but I feel that the poor, tired, overworked mothers of Great Britain need us badly.

What a very sensible Norlander Nurse Edith was! The mothers of England *did* need us properly trained nannies. Now was not the time to dwell on my heartache over Bill.

I had to pick myself up, dust myself down and, as I had done during wartime, simply get on with things. When duty calls, emotions must be put to one side, the indulgence of high emotion sacrificed.

Fortunately my job meant that I was so busy I didn't have much time to think about Bill in any case.

The twins were coming up to a year now and were toddling all over the place, their toothy little grins enchanting me every time I looked at them.

I had seen every stage of their life so far and what changes indeed! From newborns who cried and slept between feeding on demand to five-month-olds who suddenly seemed to wake up to the world, charming me with their dreamy smiles, frantically kicking little legs and curious deep blue eyes that never left mine.

Those smiling mouths were set in total determination when they reached ten months or so and realised that those same pudgy legs that were so perfect for kicking were actually quite good for standing up on too!

Of course, all children change and evolve all the time and at their own rates, but there seem to be more miracles to savour in the first year of a child's life than at any other stage. That is the wonder of children: nothing ever stands still. I urge people to remember that when they are despairing over a child who won't sleep or who is cutting a painful first tooth.

Everything is just a stage and it won't last long. Try not to despair or wish it away, as something else is always waiting round the corner to whip the rug from under your feet or charm you senseless! We can never freeze time, so we should appreciate every delicious moment of a child's life, for as we all know, they grow up so fast.

Every time I felt a stab of pain thinking of Bill, or the memory of his brown eyes drifted into my brain, I forced myself to concentrate on the children. Every bit of love I could have channelled into a relationship with Bill I poured into their upbringing instead. From wide gap-toothed grins to squeals of delight, I savoured it all.

Their chubby little arms flung enthusiastically round my neck when I gave them bedtime kisses slowly healed the hurt and dislodged the pain in my heart. And if I ever allowed my mind to wander to places it shouldn't, you could bet that a cry for nanny would soon distract me.

By the time they approached their first birthday I had filled their lives with love and they had patched over my broken heart.

All mothers are privileged to go on that journey with their child in that first precious year. Every time I have a tiny baby in my care I consider that journey to be an absolute honour. I've been asked so many times over the years what my favourite age is and I always say the same thing.

The tiny helpless newborn infant.

There really is nothing so awe-inspiring as holding a fresh young life in your arms.

How lucky I was back then to have added twins to my experience of care. Double the work it's true, but also double the fun! Seeing the world through their excitable eyes was enormously satisfying.

'You clever things,' I grinned in the nursery one morning when they pointed jubilantly with podgy little fingers to the open window.

'Brr . . . brr,' squealed Violet, jumping up and down on her bottom in excitement.

'Yes, poppet, a bird,' I smiled. 'Shall we look at the birds outside the window? There's blackbirds and blue ti . . .' Gazing out the window my voice trailed off. 'What on earth?' I gasped.

There, crawling through the rhododendron bush, were three of the most suspicious-looking youths I had ever seen. They wore trilby hats firmly pulled down over their faces, and what's more, they were crawling straight to the front door.

'Mrs Sacks!' I shrieked. 'Come and look at this.'

She rushed in, took one look out of the window and paled.

From our position upstairs we heard the sharp rap of the door handle and froze like startled rabbits.

'I don't like the look of that one little bit,' I whispered.

'It's all right, Nurse Ashford,' she said. 'I'll go.'

She rushed downstairs and I realised my heart was thundering in my chest.

'Stay here, children,' I said, softly shutting the door and straining over the banister to listen.

'Does Bob live here?' said a gruff voice.

I could tell by Mrs Sacks' voice that she was scared. 'Yes,' she said. 'He lives in the garage but we haven't seen him around for weeks.'

With that she shut the door with a bang and hurried back up the stairs.

From my vantage point I could see the men scurry up the path, furtively glancing this way and that.

'Well, what on earth was that about?' I gasped.

Carolyn shrugged, mystified.

Nothing that happened around these parts surprised me any more.

An hour later the door knocker went again and Mrs Sacks answered. This time it was two policemen.

'We are looking for three youths who have absconded from a remand home,' said one, looking past Carolyn into the corridor. 'They raided the warden's office and stole a sum of money from him. We have reason to believe they may have come to this address. They are friends with a former resident, a man who goes by the name of Bob. Do you know him?'

Oh dear, oh dear, oh dear. This was getting worse by the moment.

Carolyn ushered them into the living room and softly closed the door. I heard a muffled exchange of voices and a short while later she came out.

'Nurse Ashford,' she said. 'They are looking for people who saw anything to give a statement.'

Enough was enough. 'I am not getting involved,' I replied firmly. 'What would the Norland say? I am horrified at the thought of getting embroiled in a police investigation. The scandal. Imagine?' I blustered.

'Of course,' she soothed, returning to the policemen. 'Don't worry, I understand.'

By the time the local constables had taken their leave I had already made up my mind.

'I'm sorry, Mrs Sacks,' I said. 'But I can't continue to work here any longer and I am handing in my notice.'

Bombs, disease, rockets, evacuees, East End mothers, heartbreak even, I could handle. But this? Shady goings-on, men crawling about in bushes, and flash Harry in medallions? Far too much scandal for my stomach, thank you very much.

And so with a heavy heart and a cuddle from Violet and Peter I took my leave. The twins were as happy, healthy and robust children as you could possibly hope to meet.

I, meanwhile, was twenty-five and owing to Bill's new-found celibacy was no closer to finding love and starting my own family, but thanks to this large and hectic household my confidence as a child-carer, and in my calling, was now absolute.

I might not have the love of a man, but I had the love of many children to warm the recesses of my soul.

Of course I was disheartened to have lost out on the potential of a relationship with Bill, sadder even than I'd been when I discovered that Henry, a man I actually was in a relationship with, had cheated on me. But what doesn't kill you makes you stronger and it was time for me to move on to pastures new.

My work here was done, but what a most curious job. If this was how post-war England was shaping up, it seemed that wartime was perhaps not safer, but at least more normal!

Dramatic changes were sweeping the whole world and it was not a place I recognised any more. Bikinis had gone on sale in Paris, and the seeds of rock 'n' roll were being sown in America. Women's lives had also radically altered even in the time I had been with the Sacks.

Women were increasingly being employed in traditionally masculine jobs, not just in manual labour but in skilled positions, and the Trades Union Congress pledged itself to equal pay as a principle. They were drafted into work in key jobs in nursing, civil defence, government departments and transport. At the same time hundreds of nurseries were being established. War nurseries like the one I had worked in had paved the way for the idea of communal care in a nursery.

The Post Office and Civil Service had scrapped their marriage bar, meaning that for the first time they would employ married women. Female teachers could also continue to work after marriage and universities increasingly became open to women.

Women's talents were at last being recognised. They were entering the Royal Society as female fellows, starting their own organisations and opening doors previously shut to them. They were taking on men at their own game!

Thanks to all this, out on the streets I saw more and more women wearing trousers. Even the Church of England was relaxing its dress code and no longer required women to wear hats to attend services. Nineteen forty-six also saw the first broadcast of *Woman's Hour*.

I never frowned upon any of these dramatic changes; rather, I looked upon them like a bewildered bystander. As a Norland-trained nurse, though, I was ahead of the game in some respects and at long last childcare methods were coming into line with my own outlook.

In 1946, the American paediatrician Dr Benjamin Spock published a book on childrearing called *The Common Sense Book of Baby and Child Care*. This was a bestseller in the US and the UK and was hugely influential in changing attitudes to parenting. It challenged methods based on strict discipline and replaced spanking with communication and respect for children. A way I had been working for the past seven years, of course, in my own quiet fashion. It was a huge step forward for children and their future care.

But the big question remained: with the world changing at such a rapid and bewildering pace, could I change with it?

Testimonial

Nurse Brenda has carried her responsibility with the highest degree of skill and devotion to which the remarkable progress and robust health of her charges now bears testimony.

It is with deep and profound regret that we now release her to return to her own home. Her generous and invaluable service is sincerely appreciated and her cheerful presence in the household will be greatly missed by all.

Mrs Sacks

NANNY'S WISDOM

Take time to cheer people up

As a nanny I didn't regard childcare as my only duty. I am a human being first and a nanny second. When Mrs Sacks was terribly down and suffering with the baby blues, I took time to treat her kindly and attempt to cheer her up. I do so wish people would take the time to look around them at the people in their lives and see who could do with cheering up. Throughout my career I have always advised parents and children to pick a little bunch of flowers or make a card for a friend, partner, mother or anyone in their life whom they love and is troubled by something. It's the little things that count in life and for many people just knowing they are in someone's thoughts will cheer them up no end. Giving is infinitely more rewarding than receiving.

The Queen of Puddings

All my charges, the Sacks children included, loved it when I cooked my mother's recipe for queen's pudding. I adored it as a child and I still cook it today. It's very cheap to make but a real treat and smells delicious when it's cooking. Nothing says 'I love you' like warm meringue and jam.

4 oz (125 g) fresh white breadcrumbs
1 oz (30 g) caster sugar
1 teaspoon grated lemon rind
15 fl oz (450 ml) fresh milk
1 oz (30 g) butter

2 egg yolks
2 tablespoons apricot jam, or any other favourite jam
4 egg whites
4 oz (125 g) caster sugar, plus extra for sprinkling

Put the breadcrumbs, sugar and lemon rind in a basin and toss lightly together to mix. Pour the milk into a saucepan, add the butter and gently heat until the butter melts. Pour on to the breadcrumb mixture, stir well and leave to stand for 30 minutes. Beat the egg yolks until fluffy and then mix into the breadcrumb mixture. Spread the mixture into a well-greased ovenproof dish and bake in the middle of an oven set at 170°C (320°F) for 30 minutes, or until firm and set. Remove from the oven and spread carefully and evenly with your favourite jam whilst it's still warm.

Next, whisk the egg whites until stiff, then beat in the caster sugar until the egg whites are nice and satiny. Cover the base with swirls of meringue, sprinkle with extra caster sugar and bake for a further 20 minutes until the top is pale gold. Serve warm with cream.

Make time to talk
Put aside thirty minutes each day to sit and ask your child how his or her day was and then listen to the answer. It's not long, but that thirty minutes spent with your attention focused solely on your child will have an enormous effect.

3

The Circle of Life

The Itsy Bitsy spider climbed up the spout.
Down came the rain and washed the spider out.
Out came the sun and dried up all the rain
And the Itsy Bitsy spider went up the spout again!

Twentieth-century nursery rhyme

The contractions were coming thick and fast, and by the way missus had clenched her eyes shut and was gripping the bed sheets for dear life, another one was on its way.

The sound, almost feral in its cry, was terrifying. 'Get. The. Doctor. Nowwwwww,' she howled.

The contraction exploded within her and the pain of it almost seemed to lift her clean off the bed. The scream was so loud, I swear cows in the neighbouring field stopped chewing and stared puzzled at the window.

'This baby is coming,' she hollered, her eyes bulging as she gripped on to my hand like a vice.

'We've called the doctor out, Mrs Barclay,' blustered the elderly maternity nurse, feverishly wringing a towel in her chubby hands. 'He's on his way.'

The nurse looked at the door, then shot me a worried

look. I knew just what she was thinking. Would he get here in time?

He'd only come out to examine her not half an hour ago and as nothing was happening he'd gone off to have his lunch. What's more, he hadn't seemed best pleased to be called out again so soon.

'Aaaarrrrghhhh,' she screamed again.

'Hang in there, Mrs Barclay,' I said more calmly than I felt. 'You're doing absolutely marvellously.'

Her face screwed up in pain and I felt so helpless as she collapsed back, exhausted, on the pillow.

'That's it,' I soothed. 'Gather your strength for the next one.'

Looking at her face now I was in no doubt. This baby was coming, doctor or no doctor!

Before I'd started here two weeks previously I hadn't planned on actually witnessing the birth. The lady of the house should have given birth by now and by rights I should have been nursing a little baby, not mopping the fevered brow of a labouring woman. But then life has a funny way of turning out how you least expect, doesn't it?

Jean and Percival Barclay were wealthy pillars of the community in a pretty village in Hertfordshire. They had two children, Jane, six, and Penny, three.

The sprawling farmhouse they lived in was set in acres of beautiful grounds, and Jean was mad keen on the animals they owned: horses, pigs and cows galore. After the chaos of the Sacks household and con men crawling through the bushes, I found the peace and quiet of this tranquil countryside most welcoming.

Percival Barclay was a reticent but terribly clever chap. We didn't see him for much of the week as he had a very important job as chairman of a newspaper group in London.

Percival was typical of the men of his era. It was 1947 and during the week he seemed to live in his pinstriped suit. Weekends would be spent with his golfing buddies or locked away in his study. Even now, at the moment of his third child's arrival into the world, he was sitting downstairs puffing on a pipe and doing *The Times* crossword. He would no more dream of being here in this room than he would walk to the moon. It simply wasn't done. Men weren't to be subjected to the gruesome realities of childbirth.

In 1947 the NHS hadn't even been formed yet, though it was just around the corner, so it was left to a maternity nurse and doctor to ensure that everything ran smoothly. An emergency C-section simply wasn't an option.

Just then the door burst open and in bowled a frightfully put-out doctor. His moustache was quivering with rage as he dumped his black leather bag by the bed.

'What do you mean by calling me out again, Nurse?' he bristled. 'I was in the middle of my lunch.'

'We hate to disturb your lunch, Doctor,' I said smoothly. 'But it would appear Mrs Barclay's baby is unconcerned at whether you've eaten. She's coming now, you see.'

The red-faced doctor looked from me to Mrs Barclay, who was bearing down with a dogged determination and starting to push.

'Ah, OK,' he blustered. 'Right, you,' he said, pointing to me. 'Fetch me some hot water and towels.'

I raced downstairs and filled up as many bowls of hot water as I could. In the kitchen, Mr Barclay glanced at me over the top of his paper and nodded stiffly.

By the time I got back to the room the doctor had scrubbed up, slipped a sterile sheet under Mrs Barclay's buttocks and was examining her.

Mrs Barclay, meanwhile, wasn't waiting for anyone and was pushing with all her might, a vein on the side of her head throbbing as she bore down and grunted with the effort.

'Delivery imminent,' sighed the doctor, probably still thinking of the half-eaten steak and kidney pie growing cold on his kitchen table.

In a split second the atmosphere in the room changed from one of panic to absolute, focused calm.

Mrs Barclay had stopped screaming and now seemed almost turned in on herself, perhaps preserving every drop of energy for the arduous task ahead.

'Little pushes,' said the doctor as he crouched down and gently manoeuvred her on to her side. 'That's it, nice and slowly. Breathe deeply.'

Suddenly the room fell under a magical spell and time seemed to freeze.

The baby's head was crowning.

'Not too fast,' said the doctor. 'Pant, don't push, this baby is going to be a big one.'

I could see it. I could actually see it.

With the next contraction the head started to push through.

'Oh,' I breathed, wide-eyed with wonder. 'She's coming.'

Suddenly the head slithered out and I gasped.

What on earth?

'Oh, you're lucky,' squealed the maternity nurse. 'She's born in a caul.'

I'd heard of babies born in their amniotic sac and I'd heard a child born this way was said to possess remarkable luck or intuitive powers. Who knew whether it was simply an old wives' tale? But it was fascinating to observe.

As the rest of the baby's body slid effortlessly out on to the sheet I was stunned to see she was entirely encased in a bluey-white transparent bag. We could just see her little face gazing out, bewildered, from behind her veil.

'Boy? Girl?' cried Mrs Barclay.

'It's a healthy girl,' said the doctor. 'And she'll be fine.'

Working quickly, the doctor deftly made a small incision in the membrane by the baby's nostrils so that she could breathe, and then gently peeled back the rest of the sac from her skin.

I stood rooted to the spot, utterly spellbound. It was like watching the most precious present of all being tenderly unwrapped.

And what a gift! Now that the sac had gone I could see a wriggling little pink bundle. She was utterly perfect, from her chubby little clenched fists to her curled-up toes.

I had just witnessed birth in all its brutal, wondrous, messy splendour.

'She's utterly beautiful, Mrs Barclay,' I breathed.

I felt my eyes begin to mist over and a lump form in my throat. There really is nothing so life-affirming as watching a baby being born!

'Towel!' barked the less sentimental doctor.

Minutes later the cord was clamped and the maternity nurse weighed her.

'Ooh she's a big one,' she smiled. 'Nearly eleven pounds.'

With that Mrs Barclay went as white as flour and collapsed back against her pillow. The effort of delivering an eleven pound baby born in a caul seemed to entirely swamp her.

The nurse wrapped the baby in a towel. Apparently sensing that Mrs Barclay needed peace as the doctor delivered her placenta, she handed her to me instead.

Holding the precious bundle like it was the most fragile lace, I breathed in that incredible musky smell that all newborn babies seem to have and sighed in wonder.

Walking with her over to the window, I gently peeled back the towels so I could get a better look.

Her little face may have been covered in blood and mucus, but quite honestly she was the loveliest thing I had ever clapped eyes on.

Just then she made a slight snuffling sound and her deep blue eyes opened just a fraction for the first time. A tingle ran the length of my body as I realised I was the first person in the world she had set eyes on.

'Welcome to the world, sweetheart,' I whispered. 'You're a big girl, aren't you.'

Her blue eyes gazed curiously at me and for a split second I felt an instinctive understanding run between us.

'I'm your nanny,' I whispered, softly stroking her furrowed little brow with my finger. Her skin was as soft as satin.

Not since David's birth all those years before had holding a baby affected me quite so profoundly. I had witnessed the miracle of her birth and had the honour of holding her just minutes after she was unpeeled from her caul. It was a moment I shall treasure always.

Today, doctors and medical experts have unravelled the many complex and mysterious biological processes our bodies go through, but I don't think any have really managed to put their finger on why it is that when we see a newborn baby we are rendered speechless and sobbing. It could be something to do with hormones, or simply the wonder of seeing a fresh new life so full of promise enter this world. I prefer to appreciate it for what it truly is – *one of life's most incredible miracles*.

Seconds later my little miracle let rip a ferocious and indignant cry.

'Nothing wrong with baby's lungs then,' chuckled the maternity nurse.

Baby Pippa and I formed a strong bond in those power-ful minutes after her birth. Little Pippa and I were as close as close can be. For eight blissful years she was my be-all and end-all.

As Pippa and the rest of her fellow baby boomers grew up and took their first unsteady steps, the world was a rapidly changing place.

Nine months after her birth, on 5 July 1948 the National Health Service came into being, pledging free health care for all. It was a momentous achievement and everybody wanted the new service to work. We may still have been war-weary and accustomed to austerity, and rationing was still in place, but it was a sign of good things to come. Prior to this, only people who could afford expensive private health insurance – mainly men – could be guaranteed health care. Now it was available to everyone.

Another influence on government thinking was the 1943 'Our Towns' report by the Women's Group on Public Welfare, which called for the family to be given greater importance in the postwar rebuilding effort. It also emphasised the significance of the child guidance movement, nursery schools and closer cooperation between parents and schools.

But away from all this reform and the leaps forward in health and social care for women and children, we still preferred the simple things in life in the late 1940s. There was no television set at the Barclays', so we contented ourselves with plenty of walks in the fresh air and listening to plays on the radio. Life was certainly a lot less complicated, competitive and fast-moving, and all the better for it if you ask me.

Foreign travel was out of the reach of most people so the British seaside and Butlin's camps became a magnet for pleasure-seekers. Sometimes we would all head down to the seaside. What a thrill. The drive down would take no time in Mr Barclay's Morris Minor. There simply wasn't the same traffic on the road as there is today. On the rare occasions we did encounter traffic we played I spy to while away the time and once there we had the most glorious time paddling in the sea.

'A little of what you fancy does you good, girls,' I told them as we tucked into our ice creams.

The girls and I giggled helplessly as we watched a Punch and Judy show or hapless fathers being buried up to their necks in the sand.

As we paddled, beach-combed and built sandcastles under an endlessly blue cloudless sky, I marvelled how for the first time in years one could gaze up at the sky without fear of seeing the Luftwaffe drone into view. Barbed wire had been cleared from our beaches and Britain was once again a green and pleasant land.

The raunchy bikini hadn't hit the shores of Britain yet, so most people wore much more modest one-pieces and the same ghastly rubber hats that I had had to wear when learning to swim at Bognor all those years ago.

The girls were thrilled by the sea and loved to splash and paddle, running up to the shore's edge and then back up the beach again, shrieking with laughter when the waves crashed against their toes. Pippa was always a little more hesitant about the waves than her bigger sisters, which reminded me of one Nurse Nina Baker's story of her young charge Susan, who, when taken to the sea for the first time, toddled down and then promptly returned. 'Well, Susan,' Nurse Baker had said. 'Do you like the sea?' 'No, Nursie, barf too big,' she'd replied.

By night Mr and Mrs Barclay might go to one of the popular Italian or French restaurants that were popping up everywhere and I would stay in to look after the girls.

Most children, I find, become surprisingly active at bedtime, so as a treat on holiday we'd play snap or snakes and ladders. Yo-yos and games of 'it', which I'd seen the Bethnal Greenies play during the war, were replaced by board games and skipping ropes.

Once I'd tucked them in, the girls loved to hear tales of Christopher Robin or Toad of Toad Hall, or the *Just So Stories* by Rudyard Kipling. Looking back, those times were so innocent. The sense of community was still strong and after the carnage of war life was looking up. Britain was recovering.

Father's business, whilst not exactly booming, was at least surviving and now Christopher was helping him out. Michael was starting to train for a career in the theatre and Basil was working abroad for a timber firm. Mother, still at a loss after losing her beloved evacuees, had bought herself a dog, a delightful little whippet she called Bambi, to fuss over and care for. The baby boom was keeping midwife Kathleen rushed off her feet and she seemed to spend all her time delivering babies in Surrey.

Thanks to the Children Act of 1948, child welfare was being taken seriously, and important steps were also being made in children's health. I marvelled at how lucky and privileged we were suddenly to have access to vaccines and medicine that before just simply hadn't been available. Little Pippa and her sisters wouldn't have to go through the pain of so many childhood illnesses as I had done.

The pharmaceutical industry was creating a flood of new drugs. Penicillin, better anaesthetic agents, cortisone, drugs for the treatment of mental illness such as schizophrenia and depression, diuretics for heart failure and antihistamines, all became available. And so it seemed that innovation could be born from times of crisis.

It was on a visit to a new NHS baby clinic for a checkup for Pippa that I realised I was perhaps in danger of being viewed as an outdated relic, a pre-war dinosaur.

I was sitting in the clinic holding Pippa in my lap. She was dressed ever so smartly in her little wool coat and fur-trimmed bonnet, I was in my Norland uniform, and the older girls were playing happily nearby pulling a little wooden duck on wheels about. Jane and Penny were ever so good and on the whole were content to sit and paint pictures, do colouring-in or, like now, play with whatever toys were available.

A mother sitting nearby looked at me and sniffed. 'You one of them Norland Nannies?' she asked.

'Yes I am,' I smiled. 'Have you heard of us then?'

'Oh I've heard of 'em all right,' she laughed harshly. 'Out of touch they are with all their highfalutin ways.' She snorted again as if to emphasise her point.

'What do you mean?' I asked, feeling my cheeks flush scarlet at this sudden attack on my profession.

'What's the good in having a Norland Nanny?' she went on. 'They don't work, they don't like to get their hands or their uniform dirty. I mean to say, it's ridiculous. Who needs a nanny in a cape?'

I sat there gobsmacked, staring after the woman as she was called in to see the doctor.

Was that really how she saw me? How the world saw us? As work-shy snobs?

Furious, I took the girls, tucked Pippa up in her coach pram and marched home.

'I have never been lazy in my whole life,' I muttered as I strode down the road.

She couldn't have known any of those nannies who had worked from dawn until nightfall throughout the war with just a half-day off a week. Who had run to air-raid shelters clutching their charges in their arms. Accuse me of anything you like, but not laziness!

'What's wrong, Nana?' asked Jane, sensing the dark cloud that seemed to hover overhead.

'Nothing, darling,' I said, with as bright a smile as I could muster.

But do you know what I did as soon as I got home?

I took off my uniform, folded it up and put it away, then changed into a plain blue overall dress.

I didn't want to be seen that way.

I am sure the Norland would have had a blue fit, but the world had changed so much since 1939. As we entered the 1950s, a nanny in a uniform seemed strangely outdated.

How different things were from when I had first sat in a drafty lecture room at the Norland headquarters in Pembridge Square as a nervous new recruit listening to our principal, Miss Whitehead.

Miss Whitehead was a legendary figure and one knew better than to cross her. By accident on my first day I committed the cardinal sin of closing a window, such was my eagerness to ingratiate myself to my fellow students. She had swept in and fixed me with a look so chilly the temperature had plunged a few degrees. Her lips had pursed disapprovingly.

'Your first lecture will be on hygiene,' she'd barked. 'Will the student at the back please open the window? Fresh air makes for healthy living.'

I'd wanted the ground to swallow me up, and trust me, none of us ever dared to close a window in the presence of Miss Whitehead again.

She had only become principal four years earlier, in 1935, after working as a trained nurse and midwife, but had quickly made her mark as a draconian guardian of the uniform. She was adamant that we nurses would only be seen as superior nannies if we dressed and behaved impeccably at all times.

When I'd been training in London in 1939, stylish society ladies were just catching up with our American cousins over the pond. Two years earlier in 1937 Lana Turner had raised eyebrows in her film *They Won't Forget* in which she wore a tight sweater with her full bosom pushed up and out by a brassiere.

Out on the streets women emulated this look with tight sweaters, a slick of pillar-box red lipstick and silk stockings. Lavish Hollywood stars were influencing the way British women dressed with bias cut dresses designed to drape and flatter the contours of a woman's body or horror of horrors, backless dresses to show the tantalising curve of her spine.

Women were certainly becoming more daring and determined to show their body's best assets off. Not so in Pembridge Square!

No such daring for us Norlanders. Miss Whitehead would never have tolerated us wearing such feminine outfits. Inside the hallowed walls of the Norland there was no room for silk stockings or make-up. Make-up was strictly banned from the nursery, and stockings were made of sensible and comfortable lisle.

'I am a stickler for a properly worn uniform,' she'd reminded us time and time again. 'I might think of having a Roll of Honour of the nurses who really do wear their uniform properly, but I am afraid it would not require a large frame,' was another of her classics.

But the thing she was most fond of recounting was this: 'The uniform shows you have all entered the Norland Institute for the same purposes. You are given the uniform, having promised to wear it, that you may show to the world that you are a member of that institute which has those high ideals. Among them is the great responsibility it means to bring up little children to be true and good, to enable them to be men and women of the highest character.

'You have much to be thankful for. The first style with its long cloak was just six inches from the ground. The fastenings were a hook and an eye at the neck and three tiresome little tabs to be buttoned. The summer cloak, which was a delicate grey, showed every mark. Next came cloaks with capes down to the wrists, and when the wind was frolicsome, the nurse was enveloped in the cape, and unable to see for the moment.'

So you see, the uniform was *everything* and putting it away felt almost like a betrayal of the very training I held so dear. But then I thought of the Norland's other strongly held belief: you were there to serve the parent and you must be prepared to do everything they had to do.

I had to stay in touch with the modern mother and be seen to be supporting her, not staying stubbornly entrenched in the past. A nanny needed to be versatile. It may only have been eleven years since I'd graduated, but so much had happened it may as well have been a lifetime ago.

Since then I had put out incendiary bombs with cowpats, run from German fighter planes, narrowly avoided getting killed by flying shrapnel and battled disease and protective cockney mothers. I had changed, the world had changed and I had to be seen to be keeping pace.

Did I look back? Regret putting away the uniform that

had come to symbolise all that was unique about a Norland Nanny? Not really. I still have my beautiful blue silk charge dress and white apron trimmed with white Belgian lace for use on special occasions. It hangs with great pride in my wardrobe. I even still look longingly on photos of my fawn-coloured day uniform complete with cloak and felt hat.

But back then I did what I felt was appropriate. I could get my hands dirty with the best of them and there and then I made a vow. I could only truly call myself a proper nanny if I did everything that a mother would do.

In the case of the Barclays that meant getting my hands really dirty!

Mrs Barclay went out every day to ride her beloved horse and feed her animals, and I used to love taking the girls out on to the farm to pick buttercups and make daisy chains. But now I realised we could all do more.

'Can I help with the animals?' I ventured one spring morning after nearly four years on the farm.

'Well, yes, Nurse Brenda, that would be lovely,' Mrs Barclay said, handing me a pail. 'You can start by milking Buttercup. The relief milker's sick.'

Buttercup was what was known as a house cow. Half Guernsey and half shorthorn, she provided all the fresh milk for the household. Her deliciously creamy milk was used in Mrs Barclay's morning coffee and the children's cereal, as well as to make cream, butter and cheese.

Looking at Buttercup staring dolefully at me, I gulped. A nanny who milks, I thought. Well, one has to be adaptable in these changing times.

The children giggled as I sat on the milking stool, took a deep breath and gently prodded Buttercup's swollen udders.

Two seconds later milk sprayed everywhere and the children were in fits of laughter.

'You're supposed to get it in the bucket, Nana,' laughed Jane as milk dripped off the end of my nose.

'Practice makes perfect,' I said, diving in again.

Poor Buttercup. She stared at me patiently with those big brown eyes as I wrestled with her udders. By the time I'd finished I'd managed half a bucket and was thrilled.

'Well done, Nana,' the children cried.

After that we had the most magical day. We fed hay to the animals, helped muck out the horses and then together we skimmed the cream off the milk to make butter.

Everyone helped out. Even their two dogs, an Alsatian called Hector and a whippet called Barney, worked as a double act.

Thanks to the new buildings nearby, hundreds of rats had been disturbed and had decided to take shelter in the barn and outhouses. Hector would race in and sniff out the rats, and as they ran for the door Barney would be waiting to catch them.

'Look,' I cried, delighted, to the children. We watched them for hours until dusk finally sneaked in over the fields.

'Come on, children,' I said, taking their hands. 'Time for tea.'

As we headed home across the fields, the light of the farmhouse spilling out across the countryside, I felt a warm flush of happiness.

Country life suited me. There was no time to feel regret

at my lost loves or lament not having time to find a new man. My heart was fulfilled and I loved my job with a passion. Surely that was more important?

'I've had a lovely day, Nana,' smiled Pippa, now three, her little hand warm in mine.

'Me too,' I trilled.

Sitting in the kitchen eating hot buttered toast and jam at the end of a day spent with the children in the fresh air of the farm, I realised what a truly important lesson I was teaching them. A sense of responsibility and how to care for others aren't easily taught; they have to be demonstrated.

That night I tucked the children up in their beds, planted little kisses on their heads and wrapped up their feet in soft blankets so their toes didn't get cold, like my own mother had done all those years before.

'Sweet dreams, girls,' I smiled.

'I think you're a super nana,' whispered Penny sleepily from under her eiderdown.

Later I was snuggled up in my own bed. I may have been alone, but suddenly, with a jolt, I realised I didn't care!

I was nearly thirty now with no husband or a child to call my own, but for some reason it didn't seem to matter. The need to find a man didn't drive me in quite the same way as being the best nanny I could possibly be did.

Being on my own wasn't actually the end of the world. From what I could see, men were nothing but trouble anyway. Perhaps I was wise to leave the heartache to others?

After that, every spare minute was spent down on the farm, helping out, watching the beauty of the changing seasons and observing the centuries-old traditions of farming.

One such tradition was that of Buttercup's yearly baby. Poor cow, every year she had to be artificially inseminated and have a calf to keep her milk supply going. The baby boom was nothing new for this sweet old cow.

When I'd been with the Barclays for nearly four years, Buttercup gave birth to a frisky black and white heifer. This heifer was quite mad; she would run around the field like a bucking bronco, charging anyone who dared come near her.

It wasn't just the heifer. Half the animals on this farm seemed quite, quite mad. The geese used to chase the horse round the fields, and Percy the enormous boar regularly broke free from his sty and would rampage round the farm.

The war nursery and caring for Jimmy and the evacuees seemed tame in comparison!

On the morning of my thirtieth birthday, I woke to find that the girls had picked me a lovely bunch of wild flowers from the meadows and made me a card. I was quite touched and looked forward to the day.

Mrs Barclay had other ideas.

'Brenda, would you mind feeding Buttercup's heifer?' she asked over the breakfast table. 'The relief milker's not shown up.'

I wasn't surprised. He was scared out of his wits of that mad creature. Even the local gravedigger, who on occasion came to help out, refused to go in the field to lay out her hay.

But what sort of message would I send to the girls if I said no?

'Of course,' I said.

'Thanks, Brenda,' she smiled, returning to her paper. 'You are a treasure.'

With the girls lined up watching safely from the other side of the fence I picked up the stack of hay and quietly opened the gate to the cows' field. The mad heifer was grazing at the far end. If I sneaked in she might just not notice me.

'You are brave, Nana,' piped up Pippa, her nose pressed against the wooden gate.

Brave or stupid.

Venturing further into the field, I stealthily started to scatter the hay, hardly daring to breathe.

Just a few more minutes, then I'd be home and dry. Suddenly I felt hot breath on my neck.

'Er Nana,' cried Jane. 'RUN!'

Turning round I found myself face to face with the mad heifer. Not since the German planes had flown overhead had I felt such adrenaline pump through my body.

I hurtled through that muddy field towards the gate like a woman possessed, the mad heifer in hot pursuit.

'RUN!' whooped and hollered the girls. 'She's gaining on you . . .'

'I'm nearly—' I started to yell, then . . . 'Urghhh,' I grunted as an almighty thud hit me in the back and I felt the air rush out of my body.

Suddenly I realised. I was airborne! Flying through the air, I landed face down in the mud with an almighty splat.

Tossed into the mud by a mad beast? Some birthday this was turning out to be!

Limping back to the house head to toe in mud, the girls supporting me, I had to laugh. Children were definitely easier to deal with than animals.

Grappling with fields of mud and cowpats reminded me of a no less dramatic incident I'd had to contend with during the war.

Cowpat scandal, as I call it, happened during the Battle of Britain in my first ever job as a nanny. As a nervous fledgling nanny I had been eager to impress my new employers and to always do right by my two charges, two adorable boys by the names of Peter and Benjy. But on one occasion, on a half-day off, I hadn't been able to resist the lure of adventure.

I'd only been part of the way to my mother's house for a visit there when a commotion in a nearby field caught my attention. A couple of farmers were furiously shovelling cow dung on to the back of the truck. I wasn't sure what they were up to but it looked like an adventure. An adventure I wanted to be part of.

'What's going on here?' I'd asked breathlessly.

'Your Arnold's daughter, ain'ch you?' replied one of the men. 'An incendiary bomb's got going over at one of your boss's fields,' he'd said, gesturing to the forty-acre field with his shovel. 'We've gotta put it out before it takes hold.'

Before he'd had time to object, I'd grabbed a shovel, hitched up my skirts and jumped in the back of the truck. Seconds later, it had backed into the field.

There hadn't been much time to lose. The shattered bomb was alight and the grass around it was already on fire. Left for much longer it'd be no time before the whole field was on fire. God only knew the devastation if it spread to the village.

'Come on, boys,' I'd cried, digging my shovel deep in the steaming pile of manure.

For half an hour we'd worked steadily, racing from the truck to the bomb and shovelling manure on to the blaze. When that ran out, we'd forked up great cowpats and thrown them straight on to the flames too.

Talk about thrilling. I'd suppressed a little chuckle as I thought of what Miss Whitehead would have said if she'd seen me. After all, the Norland had never taught me the correct way to handle a cowpat! The best way to polish a smart Silver Cross pram to a high shine, how to treat croup and colic and how to instil sound virtues, manners and etiquette in little people, yes, but cowpat handling? No.

Soon more and more villagers and ARP wardens had joined us and together we'd worked shoulder to shoulder.

I'd thought of Norland's other motto: 'United we stand'. When we'd learned it all those years ago in the lecture rooms of Pembridge Square I'd had no idea that it would take on such meaning. Finally, with sweat pouring down our faces, we finished. Disaster had been averted.

By the time I'd reached Mother's, I was exhausted, smeared in sweat and cow dung but absolutely elated.

Don't get me wrong. Nurseries were lovely places and being a Norland Nurse was all I had ever wanted, but that didn't mean I didn't yearn for a bit of adventure.

Mother had rewarded my efforts with an extra big portion of pudding. Her legendary queen's pudding, which I'd feasted on throughout my childhood, had by then been replaced with poor knight's pudding, the same thing but made with stale breadcrumbs.

So you see, thanks to overcoming bombs with cowpats, con men in bushes, babies coming out like bob-sleighs and, now grappling mad heifers, life as a nanny was turning out to be anything but dull.

To everyone's relief Buttercup's wayward daughter was sold shortly afterwards, but she had certainly made it a birthday to remember.

Most people these days seem to spend their thirtieth birthday in some riotous fashion, hosting a party or going on a holiday. I can't even remember how I spent the rest of mine, but I dare say I was tucked up in bed after I put the girls to bed and sound asleep by 10 p.m., like I was most nights. I did reflect on my life, though. Thirty is rather a milestone, isn't it, and one does tend to take stock at these times.

Jane was ten, Penny seven, and Pippa four, and caring for these three little angels was my life. If I wasn't dropping the older girls at school, collecting them or helping with their homework, I was caring for Pippa and life was certainly most busy. There was not so much as a whiff of a man on the scene and quite honestly I didn't seem to find the time nor the inclination to go looking for one.

Was I unhappy about that fact? Honestly, if I searched deep inside my soul, I would have to say no. Childcare had always been my calling, I had answered this call and every day brought its own rewards. I might not have a man, but I still had plenty of love in my life. I was doing perfectly well on my own, thank you very much.

★   ★   ★

You would have thought we'd learned our lesson about working with animals from the mad-heifer incident, but some time later at a local fair the girls won a goldfish at a stall.

'Can we keep her, Nana?' pleaded Pippa. 'Can we, please?'

Staring into her beautiful cornflower-blue eyes, how could I refuse my Pippa anything?

'Go on then,' I chuckled. 'But only on the proviso you all look after her.'

Bless them. They were so proud of their little fish, Mr Wiggles, they carried him – or her – all the way home in a water-filled plastic bag.

Back in the nursery he soon had a new home in a glass tank.

'Mr Wiggles can only stay if you all clean him out once a week and remember to feed him every day.'

They were ready for the responsibility of caring for an animal and a goldfish was the perfect place to start.

The girls nodded and promised faithfully.

True to their word, they did. But one week Penny was carrying the bowl out of the nursery to the sink when disaster struck.

'Nana!' she screamed.

Mr Wiggles had made a break for freedom and had splashed right out of the bowl and was flipping about on the nursery carpet.

Pandemonium broke out.

'Help Mr Wiggles,' cried Penny.

Oh crumbs. Getting down on my hands and knees, I frantically tried to scoop him up but he was too slippery and no sooner had I got him than he flipped out of my hands.

'He's going to die, Nana,' yelped Pippa, desperate tears streaming down her sweet little face.

Eventually I got hold of him long enough to drop him back into the bowl of water.

'Thank goodness,' I sighed, sinking back against the door to catch my breath.

There was just one problem. From that day on Mr Wiggles never swam straight again. He swam only on his side!

Mr Wiggles survived, but unfortunately, in the countryside, where there's livestock there is also dead stock, as I learned to my cost one day.

'Brenda,' called Mrs Barclay one morning after I'd dropped the older girls at school and settled Pippa for a nap. 'You wouldn't be a dear and come and help me with something, would you?'

As a nanny you hear that sentence uttered from the mouths of mothers an awful lot. From collecting something from the shop to making sure you are in for a delivery man, you are often called upon to do things outside your job description. I never was asked to carry coal or eat with the servants, which the Norland handbook stipulated was against the rules, but everyday, mundane tasks were often asked of me. I always agreed. I don't say this to sound like a martyr. I was there to support the mother and so I had to be prepared to roll up my sleeves and help out. Although even I could see that what was being asked of me now was pushing the boundaries somewhat.

Following her out to the farm I was intrigued to see Fred the local gravedigger huffing and puffing as he attempted to dig a grave in a nearby field.

It had been an icy-cold night and frost coated the fields like a white blanket.

'Ground's as tough as rock,' he muttered. 'And me tongue's hanging out for a cup of tea.'

'No time for that, Fred,' snapped Mrs Barclay. 'Keep digging.'

She seemed unusually tetchy and when we reached the sty I saw why. Her prize sow, Daisy, was lying dead. Frozen solid to the floor of the sty.

'She died last night. Vet reckons its swine fever,' she sighed. 'Highly contagious. We've got to bury her quickly and disinfect the whole farm before any of the neighbouring farms get wind.'

'But how will we get her out?' I gasped. 'She's frozen solid to the floor.'

'Only one thing for it,' she said. 'Go and start boiling some kettles. We'll have to defrost her.'

I scuttled back to the house and returned soon after with a steaming hot kettle.

'Tea?' Fred asked hopefully, as I ran past with the kettle.

'Keep digging,' I called.

Back in the sty I winced as we poured boiling water over the frozen pig. Gradually she defrosted and Mrs Barclay was able to move her a little.

But there presented our next problem.

'She weighs an absolute ton,' Mrs Barclay huffed.

A dead sow is a considerable weight.

'Can't we just call the vet?' I asked.

'No, Nurse Brenda,' she said. 'He won't come out for fear of contamination. This is down to us.'

Last I'd heard this wasn't in my job description, but it didn't seem the time to start quibbling.

'I've an idea,' Mrs Barclay said, her eyes lighting up. 'Go and get the children's sledges.'

Shaking my head, I did as I was asked and returned with a large toboggan.

'Now,' she said. 'You push and I'll pull.'

With an almighty grunt, I pushed, but as Daisy was still a bit icy she just shot straight on to the sledge and off the other side, landing with a thud by Mrs Barclay's feet.

'Oh this is ridiculous,' she cried, pushing the slippery sow and sending her ricocheting back over to me.

I felt like we were playing ping-pong with a dead pig!

Suddenly the absurdity of the situation hit me and I started to laugh. It began as a little chuckle, but soon my body was racked with laughter and tears streamed down my face.

'This is absurd,' I screeched.

'It is rather, isn't it?' Mrs Barclay said, her mouth starting to twitch.

Soon we were both in hysterics. How we got that frozen pig on to the toboggan and out across to the field, I'll never know, but the sight of two cackling women pulling a dead pig on a sledge was almost too much for poor Fred.

'Queer folk,' he muttered, putting his spade down and getting out of there as fast as he could.

Fortunately, he had dug enough of a hole for us to fit her in.

'On my count of three, tip her in,' said Mrs Barclay. 'One . . . two . . . three . . . Heave ho.'

We lifted the sledge and with a thud Daisy landed half in and half out the grave. Her little pink trotters poked out of the ground.

'Oh this is ridiculous,' I cried. 'There's only one thing for it.'

I jumped in on top of her and with a slither she landed in the bottom of the grave.

Without exchanging a word, Mrs Barclay pulled me out of the grave. Working quickly, we covered Daisy in a sack of quicklime, filled in the grave and hurried back to the house.

We never spoke again about the dead-pig incident. It remained a secret between us.

I have done many bizarre things in my career as a nanny, but that may well go down as one of the oddest.

While I was grappling in graves with frozen pigs, my contemporaries in Britain and America were spending their free time in no less energetic ways.

Across the Atlantic, rock 'n' roll had been created. With its roots in blues, jazz and gospel music, it exploded on to the scene in Britain in the mid-1950s. The 'King of Rock 'n' Roll' was one Elvis Presley. Women went crazy for his hip gyrations and men tried to emulate his cool. Both across the pond and over here women danced and strutted their stuff in fuller skirts, colourful heels and nylon stockings.

In 1952 the first record sales chart in the UK was published. Until then, success had been measured by the sales of sheet music. A year later, '(How Much Is) That Doggie in the Window?' was a hit for Lita Roza, making her the first woman artist to top the UK charts.

Nineteen fifty-three also saw the publication of *Sexual Behavior in the Human Female* by the American author and sex therapist Alfred Kinsey, and it caused huge controversy. It seemed women were having sex and what's more, enjoying it!

But while my contemporaries were blazing a trail and making front-page news for their antics, I stayed more firmly entrenched in the nursery than ever.

I don't wish to sound like a stick-in-the-mud, but those times seemed simply to wash over me. While many my age started wearing denim jeans – that symbol of teenage rebellion TV shows – cropped pants and halter-neck dresses, I stuck resolutely to my cotton dresses nipped in at the waist with a belt. What was the point of wearing racy clothes? I would never have managed to care for my charges wearing a halter-neck or tight trousers!

I had also entirely missed out on a whole new phenomenon. Children no longer simply turned into young adults once they reached eighteen, they now became *teenagers* first. But while they and their music may have been taking over the world in other places, here in the small Hertfordshire village where I lived, country music was the only sound that rang out.

It was less shake, rattle and roll and more do-si-do. Every Friday night in the next village along from ours they held country-dance lessons in the village hall. After the children went to bed I would catch the bus. I wasn't going there to meet a man; more because I loved to dance. But if there happened to be a man as lovely as Bill, then that would be rather nice too, thank you very much.

Sadly, when I pushed open the creaky door to the drafty village hall one Friday evening after I had tucked the girls up in bed, my heart sank. The place was full of couples and I was on my own!

I was just about to turn on my heel and head for home when the instructor spotted me. 'Oh don't go,' he said. 'I'm Keith, I'll partner you.'

Keith's eyes roamed over my body as he took me by the waist and guided me to the dance floor.

'We don't often get new faces here, Brenda,' he said, pressing his face so close to mine I could smell what he'd had for dinner. 'A woman like you needs special attention.'

I smiled awkwardly. I found Keith's close attention to me somewhat unnerving.

Keith ran the weekly country-dance lessons and was fairly adamant that I needed extra tuition. Unfortunately, Keith was what you might call the sexy type and his hands were forever wandering where they shouldn't have ventured.

No matter. I'd dealt with a few frisky animals back at the farm. I could deal with a harmless letch like Keith.

Week after week Keith insisted on partnering me, leaving his poor wife Kathy sitting on the sidelines. Keith seemed to have more arms than an octopus and could swing me round and do the do-si-do, all while letting one slightly clammy hand run down the small of my back.

At the end of one class Keith managed to wheedle out of me that I had that Sunday afternoon off. 'Oh you must come for tea,' he oozed. 'Kathy and I would love to have you.'

I couldn't see the harm in it. His wife would be there, after all. I felt bad refusing. Besides, Keith was a man who didn't really seem to be able to take no for an answer.

I called Mother. 'You don't mind if I don't come home this Sunday afternoon, do you?' I asked.

'Of course not, darling,' she exclaimed. 'I have Bambi to keep me company and your father and I are going to take him for a long walk.'

That Sunday afternoon, instead of returning home to the warmth of my family, I brushed my hair, splashed water on my face and headed to Keith and Kathy's with a small bouquet of daffodils.

Keith answered the door. Two things struck me immediately as I followed him into the lounge: the overwhelming stench of Old Spice and the distinct absence of his wife.

'Kathy had to go out,' he smiled as he sat on the settee and licked his thin lips. 'Her mother's sick. So afraid it's just you and I.' He patted the seat. 'Come and sit next to me.'

Perched on the edge of the sofa, I felt as out of place as Mr Wiggles the goldfish must have done when he found himself floundering about on the carpet.

As I nibbled on a crab-paste sandwich and mentally planned my escape, it appeared Keith had other things on his mind.

'There's a big competition on in London soon,' he smiled, his eyes glittering with mischief. 'You know you're good enough to enter, Brenda, with some extra tuition from myself, of course.'

With that he laughed heartily and clamped a hand down on my thigh. Dropping my sandwich I jumped to my feet.

'I won't get the time off, Keith,' I blustered.

A loaded silence hung in the air.

'Well, it's been lovely, and I'm so sorry to miss Kathy, really I am, but I best be getting back to the farm,' I said.

'Shame,' sighed Keith. 'I'll run you home.'

'Really,' I said. 'It's no bother.'

'I insist,' he smiled, staring at my bosom.

As he got his coat I looked round at the sitting room of the small semi-detached house. Pictures of Keith and his wife Kathy on their wedding day looked down from the walls.

What was wrong with some men? Did he honestly think I would fall into the arms of a married man? What did he take me for? He was as fake and cheap as the nylon shirt he was wearing.

As we bumped along the roads in Keith's Ford, I had an ominous feeling I knew what was coming. He pulled to a halt outside the farmhouse.

With no street lamps it was pitch-black inside and outside the car, but I could see the whites of Keith's eyes eyeing me up.

Suddenly he lunged across the car and pressed his thin lips on mine.

'Oh Brenda,' he groaned, his hands snaking over my body.

'Oh no you don't,' I snapped, disentangling myself from his clammy embrace.

I shot out of the car like my heels were on fire and ran like a whippet up the drive.

Once inside I ran upstairs to the landing window, my heart thumping in my chest. I saw Keith gun up his engine and speed off down the country road. Of all the disgusting, slimy . . .

I undressed, got into bed, and stared at the ceiling.

What was wrong with me? I wasn't a bad person.

'I give up,' I sighed. The only man I'd ever really felt anything for had promised himself to Jesus and all the rest seemed to be fickle cheats.

After that I had less and less time off. Mrs Barclay, suffering with a kidney problem after a nasty kick from a heifer, more often than not took to her bed when I was due a day off.

I was given time to attend one special occasion, though. Even Mrs Barclay couldn't have turned down my request for tea . . . *with the Queen Mother*.

My hands had trembled when I'd opened the smart cream envelope and seen the sender's address: St James's Palace.

'What is it, Nana?' asked Pippa. 'It looks very important.'

'Well it is rather,' I replied. 'I've been invited for tea.'

'Who with?' she asked, wrinkling her little freckled nose and peeking inquisitively over the top of the letter.

'The Queen Mother,' I gasped.

I read out loud: 'The Council of the Royal National Pension Fund for Nurses invites you to a party at St James's Palace at which Queen Elizabeth, the Queen Mother, has graciously signified her intention of being present.'

'But I can't go,' I said. 'Who will look after you girls?'

'I will,' said Mrs Barclay, walking into the room. 'You can't possibly miss this. It's not everyone's Nana who gets a royal audience.'

I giggled nervously. She was right, of course. Gracious, the Queen Mother no less.

The day of the tea party, 6 July 1954, dawned a bright, sunny, clear day, a day full of promise. It was hard to say who was more excited, me or the girls.

'Remember every detail, Nana,' piped up Penny.

'Oh do, Nana,' said Jane. 'See if she'll let you try on her crown.'

'I don't think she'll let me do that,' I chuckled. 'Now, how do I look?' Smoothing down my skirt and adjusting my belt nervously, I suddenly felt as giddy as if I were back at Pembridge Square again, a nervous new recruit about to go through pram parade.

'You look very smart, Nana,' said Penny. 'You're wearing your uniform again.'

It might seem strange to suddenly put back on the uniform I'd relegated to the back of the closet, but I could hardly go for tea with the Queen Mother at the palace in my civvies, now could I? I was representing the Norland, after all.

Just after 2.45 p.m. I found myself walking towards St James's Palace, and was soon joined by a steady stream of women, mostly in uniform. Some wore the outfit of an NHS matron, others were clearly midwives, some came from private nanny colleges like the Norland. There were district nurses, hospice nurses and ward sisters. It was a veritable army of nurses, all in slightly different uniforms, but all clad in stout shoes and all marching on the palace.

It was an impressive sight to behold and I felt proud to be amongst their number.

If the Queen Mother suddenly took ill, she would certainly not be short of medical attention!

Once inside we were ushered up a sweeping staircase to the state apartments. En route we passed many wondrous things, including a room, which contained the Mortlake tapestries, and a striking fireplace with the initials 'H' and 'A', Henry and Anne, joined in a lovers' knot. From here we entered the Queen Anne Drawing Room. Beautiful paintings covered the walls and nervous nurses stood huddled in little groups.

All too soon I was joined by another Norlander, by the name of Molly, then Eleanor . . . and Dorothy . . . Soon we were fourteen strong and shrieks of laughter and happy chatter filled the air as we caught up on Norland gossip. Being a nanny is often a lonely life and the chance to catch up with one's fellow nurses was a welcome respite.

In fact, we were so busy chatting that we barely noticed an orchestra strike up in the corner, but once it began the first bewitching chords of the national anthem, the room fell silent, frozen under a magical spell. Every nurse in the room stood ramrod straight and you could have heard a pin drop. The Queen Mother had arrived.

She was as tiny as a little bird but rarely have I seen someone with such a captivating presence.

During World War Two Elizabeth was someone who I, and the rest of the nation, admired immensely. She never once left London, not even when the dreaded German bombers were raining bomb after bomb down on our heads. She stayed put, never complained and never left her husband the King's side, despite being advised to do so. I admire the virtues of loyalty immensely and this indomitable lady showed loyalty and bravery by the bucket load.

In public there was no questioning her devotion to her people. During the Blitz she toured endless bombsites and even went to the most dangerous and worst hit place of all, the East End. What she witnessed there must surely have touched her for when Buckingham Palace was bombed she was reported to have said: 'I'm glad we've been bombed. It makes me feel I can look the East End in the face.' She worked tirelessly throughout the entire war and seemed, at least in my eyes, to embody all that was great about the bravery, guts and spirit of great British women. Hitler was said to have called her 'the most dangerous woman in Europe' because of her effect on British morale.

But watching her now, working the room in a most becoming dress of organdie patterned with cornflowers and a wide-brimmed white hat, also decorated with cornflowers, her blue eyes twinkling almost as much as the pearl and diamond necklace round her neck, it was quite hard to imagine her as dangerous. At almost fifty-four years old, she was now the nation's favourite grandmother.

Her gracious manner as her lady-in-waiting presented her to certain guests was most bewitching.

'I am so grateful you could come today,' she smiled at a senior Great Ormond Street nurse. 'I think what you do is beyond all praise.'

The stern matron melted into her sensible shoes.

Elizabeth had become the Queen Mother just two years earlier, after the death of her beloved husband. As I watched her now, charming everyone with the same empathy she had shown when picking her way through East End bomb sites, I marvelled at her stamina. She could so easily have retired from public duties and become consumed with grief, and yet here she was shaking hands and greeting nurses like a woman half her age. In fact, she was busier as queen mother than she had been as queen.

Filled with awe, I suddenly knew with an absolute certainty that this was a woman I must emulate. She hadn't stopped working, and nor must I!

'Apparently she's looking after Prince Charles and Princess Anne while Queen Elizabeth is touring the Commonwealth,' whispered Nurse Dorothy beside me.

'Then in a sense she's a nanny just like us,' I grinned.

And then suddenly she was standing within touching distance. I didn't dare invite conversation, but she smiled as she looked me up and down, taking in my smart uniform.

'What's that uniform?' I saw her mouth to her lady-in-waiting.

'Oh she's a Norland Nanny, Ma'am,' came the reply.

She fixed those penetrating blue eyes on me, smiled and nodded. 'Very good,' she said.

A buffet tea was served in the picture gallery. A wonderful spread awaited, including the largest strawberries and raspberries I've ever seen. All too soon it was time to leave, but a last treat was in store as we walked back past the Throne Room to see the Queen's Throne Chair standing beneath the canopy.

On the train back home to my beloved girls, I reflected on my day. Loyalty, duty and love were the bywords that had governed the Queen Mother's life. She had never complained, just stoically got on with her duties. I might not be terribly fashionable, I might not have a husband to call my own, but suddenly I knew with a certainty that what I was doing *counted*. Caring for little children and helping to give them the best possible start in life mattered. The Queen Mother must have made many sacrifices along the way in the name of duty. So too would I.

Loyalty, duty and love. They were what counted.

A week later, my exciting brush with royalty was put in the shade when the July edition of the *Norland Quarterly* newsletter arrived.

It contained a letter from one Nurse Anne Chermside, whose experience with royalty was somewhat more exciting than my own. Nurse Chermside had been inside the royal palace in Cairo in January 1952 when mass rioting began, signalling the beginning of the Egyptian revolution and the end of the monarchist era. Her letter was gripping.

I had been employed to look after King Farouk's youngest daughters, Princess Fadia, then aged 22 months. There were two other older daughters, Princess Ferial and Princess Fawzia. They were in the charge of a French governess, who is my great friend.

It was like a dream going from war-weary England in 1945 and working in a day nursery to sunny Egypt.

The Princesses led simple lives, school in the mornings, while I took the baby in the garden, and in the afternoons they played in the huge grounds and had friends to tea, including Crown Prince Constantine and the Princesses Sophie and Irene of Greece. In January 1952, at Abdeen Palace, I was present at the birth of Crown Prince Fouad, whom I took charge of immediately. The baby was just ten days old when, at midday, the riots and burning of Cairo began. The little Prince was put in his carri-cot and I hurriedly filled a suitcase with his clothes and tins of dried milk.

All through that fateful day the sky grew steadily darker with the smoke from the burning town, and ashes began falling on the Palace balconies – gunfire could be heard all around us. For the next two nights I slept on the nursery floor in my uniform, with a machine-gun post just under the nursery window. In three days everything was quiet, but the feeling of safety never really returned.

In June of that year we moved to Alexandria and just over a month later I was awakened at 1 a.m., told to pack a suitcase, and have the baby ready as soon as possible. This was really the beginning of the end.

King Farouk drove Queen Narriman, the baby and myself through the dark streets of Alexandria during the curfew until we had reached the palace of Ras el-Tin, which stands on the edge of the harbour about 14 miles away.

In the morning, after a night that seemed to me would never end, the Princesses, with their governess, joined us. Throughout that day things were becoming more serious.

Early on Saturday morning, 26 July, we were looking at the peaceful scene across the harbour, when suddenly there were bursts of machine-gun fire. We hurriedly closed the shutters and moved inside. The Army had surrounded the Palace during the night. We were prisoners. The Princesses were wonderful and showed not the slightest bit of fear.

At mid-day King Farouk signed his abdication in favour of his baby son and we were told to pack and be ready to leave by 6 p.m. As all our belongings were in the other Palace and in Cairo (and still are to this day) this was not difficult.

It was with sorrowful farewells and with feelings of great regret that we stepped off the quay and were taken to the Royal yacht, the *Mahroussa*. The most moving scene was the Royal Standard being taken down over the Palace for the last time. Half-an-hour later we watched the shores of Egypt disappear behind us.

From there we went to Capri, where the harbour was black with spectators, and so it was all the way to our hotel.

For many days afterwards the photographers had cameras with telescopic lenses trained on our windows. There were reporters everywhere, and some of the stories they published made me very angry – a pity the press cannot always tell the truth.

I was not without my own personal sorrow at this time, for I heard my mother had died the day we landed at Capri. We stayed on this island for three months. Gracie Fields became a great favourite with the Princesses. She was so kind to us all and we loved it when she invited us into her house and sang to us all her old and new favourite songs.

After Capri we moved to mainland Italy in 1952 and we have been here ever since. My little charge Ex-King Fouad II is now two and a half; he is a lovely little boy with fair, curly hair. Princess Ferial is now nearly 16 years old. She would very much like to be a Nursery Nurse and

I am teaching her the Norland methods. My first 'baby' Princess is now ten and quite a schoolgirl.

This is a very brief sketch of my work during the past few years. I cannot tell you of all the interesting people I have met, the places I have seen, the joys and anxieties it has brought to me, but I have never regretted a single moment of it, and count myself lucky to have been present at historical moments like these. I have seen quite a bit of the world and do not think my travels are over yet.

With my best wishes to all Norland Nurses everywhere.

What did I conclude on reading this letter? Nannies really do get to see everything of life at every single possible level, from war nurseries right up to palaces. And like Nurse Chermside, I too felt my travels were not quite over yet.

Finally, after seven years down on the farm, I started to get itchy feet. This place had been wonderful. I simply adored my charges, and my hands-on approach with the animals had made for some memorable occasions, but I felt instinctively that it was time to move on.

The magical wind of change was blowing my way, making me restless and uprooting me. There were babies being born everywhere, babies that needed my care.

I had done my duty here. I had even earned my badge of merit from the Norland in 1953 for more than five years' faithful service to one family. It was the same year that Her Majesty Queen Elizabeth had had her coronation. She had found her vocation and I mine.

It seemed I wasn't alone. Norland Nannies around the world were finally being awarded and recognised for their services to childcare.

I learned, through the *Norland Quarterly*, that an old Norlander, Kathleen Wanstall, had been given a frightfully important-sounding title by Prince Rainier III of Monaco, who went on to to marry Grace Kelly. Kathleen was no longer just Kathleen Wanstall. She was now Chevalier de l'Ordre de Saint-Charles, no less.

'My brother Prince Rainier has just made our Nana, Chevalier de l'Ordre de Saint-Charles,' wrote Princess Antoinette de Monaco. 'She has been with us since we were born and is now raising my own children. The distinction he has conferred upon her is the highest in the land and has given much pleasure to the Monégasques. She has always been close to our sides and richly deserves this reward for her love and devotion to our family.'

How very sensible the Monaco royal family were to employ such a loyal and devoted Norlander.

They weren't the only European royals to take a Norlander to their heart. Kate Fox, of whose recent sad death we had all been informed via the newsletter, had been nanny to Princess Marina, later the Duchess of Kent, Princess Olga and Princess Elizabeth. On one occasion the family were guests at the sultan's palace in Constantinople, where they dined on gold plates. Afterwards, the Sultan, so impressed with the Norland Nurse, invested her with a royal order.

Mine may not have had a royal stamp of approval, but I was every bit as proud of my badge of merit, and who knew, perhaps one day, like Kathleen Wanstall, who helped raise Prince Rainier III and his nieces and nephews, I too might have the honour of raising two generations of the same family.

But now, instinct told me, it was time to move on. It wasn't time to settle . . . not yet. Not now. Pippa was seven and although she was the apple of my eye, even I could see she needed me less and less.

Jane, now fourteen, and Penny, ten, were just as distraught as their sister.

'Please don't go, Nana,' they cried when they heard I had handed in my notice. 'Who will help us milk Buttercup?'

'I'm sorry, my darlings,' I said sadly. 'We will always stay in touch.'

I had had a riot, but it was time to move on. As I dried the tears from Pippa's blue eyes, I thought back to the magical moment I first saw her open them and gaze back at me. What a very special journey we had been on together.

Sadly, Pippa's journey was to end before my own. We did indeed stay in touch, and she grew up to be a fine young woman with two daughters of her own. I visited her many times in her own home and revelled in watching her grow as a woman and as a mother. I have always tried my hardest to stay in touch with all my families and visit them as often as time and circumstances permit. If I can't visit, I will always put pen to paper and write, and so was the case with Pippa.

Tragically, though, she was diagnosed with breast cancer and died in 2007 aged sixty. As I sat at her funeral and watched her coffin being lowered into the ground, I was struck with a deep sadness. I had been privileged to witness her entry into the world and I watched bewildered as she left it. I had gazed in awe as she had emerged blinking from her mother's womb. I had heard her first words, witnessed her first steps, tended to her grazed knees and dried her tears. And now she was gone.

'Ashes to ashes, dust to dust,' intoned the minister and I bowed my head in respect. I had witnessed the full circle of life, from birth through to death.

Life on the farm taught me a great many things. That our journey through life can be fleeting and we none of us are masters of our destiny. We are just as fragile as the snowdrops that push up through the soil in spring. We owe it to ourselves to live each day on earth as if it is our last.

Testimonial

Nurse Brenda has been in entire charge of my three children. Her care of the baby during infancy is beyond all praise and her management of all three children is admirable. It is with a feeling of real loss that she has left us to return to babies. Not only is she an outstanding nurse but her kindness and devotion to our family is beyond praise. She holds a unique place in our family life and will always be considered a member of it.

Mrs Barclay

NANNY'S WISDOM

The passage of time

When we are young we think we will remain that way for ever, that somehow we will escape the ageing process. Working at the Barclays' made me appreciate the passage of time; the passing of the seasons and that time doesn't stand still for anyone. We aren't invincible or ageless, we are but tiny specks on this great planet and we must strive to make our mark on it the best we can. More importantly than anything, we must appreciate this life and not waste a single precious moment of it. It is a cliché, but life really is a gift. Don't overplan it or complicate it by forever thinking of tomorrow. Enjoy today, for what else is there?

Make your own butter

Few people realise how easy it is to make your own butter, like we did at the Barclays'. When the girls and I used to make it we churned it by hand using Buttercup's fresh creamy milk and then squeezed it into shape on butter pats. Nowadays it's even easier.

Simply pour four pints (2.5 litres) of double cream into a bowl and whisk until thick in a blender. Continue whisking until the whipped cream collapses and separates into butterfat. This should take about five minutes. Turn the mixture into a sieve and drain off the buttermilk, using a spoon to push the mixture down and force out the fluid. Beat the remaining butter until more buttermilk separates. Drain and repeat. Wash the remaining mixture in very cold water, shape into a pat, wrap in greaseproof paper and chill in fridge. Add salt if you like the taste. It's absolutely delicious on hot toast.

Praise where praise is due!
How wonderful is it to be praised for a job well done. I still remember the utter pride I felt in being made deputy head girl for devotion to duty and ability when I was training at the Norland Institute. It's the little things that count and a kind word and encouragement in a child's ear can last a lifetime and go a long way to making a confident and secure adult. When accompanied by a kiss, a hug or even just a pat on the back, that praise will be felt a million times more deeply.

That said, I do hear some parents going overboard and virtually cheering their children for things they are supposed to be doing anyway. I do think you can take it too far. But if your child has worked hard, demonstrated a spectacular handstand or just drawn a lovely picture, then tell him or her so! Good deeds and hard work deserve *your* praise. The next time they come to tackle a difficult task it will feel all the more bearable. Hard work pays off – even if you are doing something you don't want to be doing (like laundry or making the bed).

4

The End of an Era

> Pat-a-cake, pat-a-cake, baker's man.
> Bake me a cake as fast as you can;
> Pat it and prick it, and mark it with B,
> Put it in the oven for baby and me.
>
> > Seventeenth-century
> > English nursery rhyme

Seven thirty a.m., August 1956. Courtfield Gardens, South Kensington, London, in the royal borough of Kensington and Chelsea.

I had just arrived at my new home and was about to report for duty. What a magnificent place to lay my hat!

The square of beautiful Georgian townhouses centred on a private garden spoke of money and refined elegance.

It was a thoroughly British abode, a stone's throw from Buckingham and Kensington Palaces and the even smarter districts of Mayfair and Knightsbridge.

The Clean Air Act had just been passed by Parliament in response to London's Great Smog of 1952, which killed 12,000 poor souls. For the first time in years the air felt clean and fresh. Previously, you might not even have been able to see the lampposts that dotted the square through the pea-soup fogs that would cloak London in a thick green layer of smog.

It may have been August, but a light drizzle fell over the square and it felt most refreshing on my face. Setting down my leather case on the white stone steps leading up to the front door, I shook out my umbrella and sighed happily.

The Conservatives had won back power from Labour in 1951 and taxes were low. London was booming and industry was thriving for the first time since the war. British factories churned out cars in their millions; steel and coal production was soaring; and further to the east of London the docks employed thousands of men all toiling ceaselessly. Huge ocean-going vessels loaded with produce sailed majestically in and out of the bustling docks.

London felt like the centre of the world.

Women continued to gain power and strength around the world as more and more countries granted them the right to vote.

The National Childbirth Trust (NCT) had recently been established. Up until then women were given little or no information about pregnancy and birth and just blindly followed their doctor's instructions. Now, for the first time, they had support, advice and guidance. Ultrasound scans were just around the corner and a woman didn't have to needlessly suffer a life-threatening birth. She could have a caesarean section instead!

Here in South Kensington, however, there were no sexual revolutions, civil-rights movements or record-breaking attempts made, that I knew of! Genteel peace and prosperity prevailed. The only sound was the clanking of glass milk bottles as a milkman tootled past standing up inside his refrigerated truck.

'Good morning to you, ma'am,' he smiled, politely tipping his little white cap in deference to me.

'And a good morning to you too, sir,' I beamed back. People were so polite and courteous in those days. It was commonplace to greet a stranger like a friend.

From inside the mansion, however, a different greeting drifted down the steps to meet me. The distinctive mewing cry of a newborn baby rang out and I smiled.

Before I knocked on the imposing door, I took a moment to pause and reflect on my purpose here.

I was to be nanny to two-week-old twin girls and help their poor exhausted mother. I was here to make this the happiest home it could possibly be. Since leaving the Barclays fifteen months previously I had already stayed in four private homes, three caring for young children and the fourth looking after two young boys so that their parents could go on a skiing holiday. With each job I had become aware of a growing need inside me.

I started in a home where the mother was frazzled, burnt out and in dire need of help. I left behind me, I hoped, a happier, more fulfilled home.

I can't have been doing too badly as word had got round that I was open to short-term bookings and now I was booked solid with short placements for new mothers for the next nine months!

This was my new calling. Nowadays you would call it trouble-shooting, but back then I liked to call it good old-fashioned common sense from Nanny.

Going from home to home to get new mothers on their feet was teaching me so much. With each home and family I worked for I realised that what I loved more than anything was getting the family on its feet and creating the happiest home I possibly could.

Sprinkling a little of the magic I had experienced in my own childhood was proving most gratifying. I had enjoyed a blissful childhood and a home life filled with love, laughter and warm, rich cooking smells.

I had puzzled many times over the ingredients for the perfect recipe for a happy home. It needed to be a place with parents who worshipped their offspring. Throw in some stability, a dash of routine and respect. Sprinkle some fun and imaginative games and stir well.

A vital ingredient in this recipe, I had since concluded, was the mother. As long as the mother is happy, the household will be happy. The mother truly is the heart and soul of a family. So why, I reasoned now, couldn't I recreate that recipe in homes around Britain?

I wasn't alone in my thinking. Sir Paul Dukes wrote in the *Norland Quarterly*:

The fundamental and basic unit of society is the home. In the cold war in which, unfortunately, the world is at present plunged, and where the issues are between two forms of society, one democracy and one totalitarianism, it is interesting to follow what the Russians do about the matter of the family. Even in Russia the family has been restored to a certain place in society. That is the law of nature and people will bring disaster upon themselves if they persist upon placing a political ideology in precedence to the family, persisting that a child should be brought up a good Marxist sooner than he should be brought up to be a good son to his father and mother.

Indisputably it is the woman who makes the home and not the man. It is the woman who makes in a family the peculiar sense of people belonging to each other.'

I agreed wholeheartedly. The mother is everything in a home, without a happy mother there is no home. Just a house.

Were my opinions isolated from society? Not in the slightest. Magazines in the 1950s were full of articles encouraging women to return to their traditional roles as homemakers. They promoted the idea that feminine virtues were most important and that motherhood was the most important role a woman could occupy. I agree with this.

I am all for a woman working if that is what her heart desires; one must follow one's heart after all. But whether a mother is in a part-time or a full-time role, she must be happy if the home is to be full of contentment and love.

After all, the world would be a much happier place if people tried to fill their houses with love. Some people just needed a little reminding, that's all.

With that I rapped the heavy black lion's-head knocker on the mansion door twice.

The man of the house was one Mr Gordon. He was a consultant obstetrician and gynaecologist. Mr Gordon was a man of few words but, as I was later to find out, he was possessed of a kind heart that would come to my rescue.

'Do come in,' he said gruffly. 'Babies this way.'

He led me through to the day nursery, where the new mother was sitting with her twins.

'Oh I say,' I breathed. 'Aren't they beautiful? You must be so proud.'

'Yes,' murmured the quite clearly exhausted woman.

'Now,' I said, smiling cheerfully, taking off my summer coat, folding it carefully and putting it out of sight. 'Let's get one thing straight right away. I don't know what you've heard of Norland Nannies, but I am here to do whatever you need me to do. Whatever you would do in the house, I must be prepared to do; be that wiping down the kitchen, doing the ironing, feeding the baby or making a cup of tea. I am here to serve you. Happy mother, happy babies, I always say.'

Her eyes suddenly grew as wide as saucers. 'Really?' she gasped. 'Oh what a relief.'

'And we'll start now,' I said, rolling up the sleeves of my white summer overall dress. 'What would you like me to do?'

'Well,' she said, her face wrinkling into a frown. 'I'm getting in a muddle with their feeding times. It's so hard to keep track. This beastly baby brain. I can't make head nor tail of things at the moment.'

'Don't worry,' I laughed. 'You're not alone.'

I wasn't the least bit surprised to hear this. All new mothers struggle with getting their babies into a regular feeding pattern.

I pulled out a notepad and paper.

'Four-hourly is the best way from my experience, and as it can be so tricky to keep track of, particularly with twins, we can write it down here. Are you breast- or bottle-feeding?'

'Oh bottle-feeding,' she exclaimed, as if there couldn't possibly be any other way.

I wasn't much surprised to hear that either. Most of the mothers I came across in those days seemed to want to bottle-feed instead of breastfeed. I encouraged them to try breastfeeding and if they didn't like it to use the bottle, but I never pushed it either, especially not if they were adamant. That wasn't my job; besides, as every good nanny knows, you aren't there to pass comment or judge. Women make their own decisions, the ones they feel are right for them.

I had a sneaking hunch it had something to do with the war. During those terrible years women had lived with so many restrictions hanging over them – rationing, followed by blackouts. Life had been one long rule book.

Now the war was over and women were enjoying their freedom. Women's lives and expectations were being transformed before my very eyes. They wanted to be out at coffee mornings or bridge clubs or golfing with their friends, and breastfeeding does curtail you somewhat. Besides which, bottle-feeding was even easier now.

During the war years the government had introduced national dried milk for all bottle-fed babies. It was so easy to make up. When I'd trained at Great Ormond Street before the outbreak of war I'd got in the most terrible muddle trying to make up formula feed from different quantities of milk, water, sugar, lactose or glucose. Now it was even easier for women to bottle-feed and from what I could see, the ladies I worked for wouldn't have it any other way.

'I'll show you the twins' nursery,' said Mrs Gordon, leading me up the corridor.

Back in the 1950s parents never slept with their babies. Co-sleeping simply didn't exist and babies were mainly put straight into their own nursery from birth. Nowadays, the thinking is drastically different and it's recommended that babies sleep with their mothers in the same room for the first six months, but back then that was simply the way it was. Parents didn't worry as much and monitors, alarms and video link-ups hadn't yet been dreamed up. I didn't worry about the children being in another room, but I was concerned I might not hear them when they woke.

'If it's OK with you I'd rather have them in with me,' I said. 'That way I can hear them when they wake for a feed.'

'You'll feed them in the night?' she asked, simply agog.

'Like I say,' I replied smoothly. 'I must be prepared to do whatever you do. I do think it's best for Mother to do the ten p.m. feed, though, with the father. It's so important for bonding and often the only time Father sees the child if he works, but I am happy to do the rest of the feeds.'

She nodded enthusiastically.

'And now,' I smiled. 'How about we make you a nice cup of tea and you go back to bed for a nap. New mothers need their rest, you know.'

Gratefully she handed me the twins. 'Thank you, Nurse Brenda,' she said.

'Just doing my job,' I replied.

And so there in Courtfield Gardens, South Kensington, we all settled into our new roles.

Over the coming days I hung back, watched and listened. Every new mother is different and using my instincts I tried to get the feel of the house so I could be super-sensitive to its balance and rhythms.

I was always thinking . . . thinking and watching. In many ways a good nanny must be like a mind-reader.

What does Mother like? How does she like to do her washing, fold her clothes, hold her baby? Does she want me in the room or is she craving space to bond with her babies?

And the same goes for babies. No two babies, including the twins I was caring for now, are alike. Some love to be stroked; others are super-sensitive to touch and would rather be left alone. Some will sleep at the drop of the hat; others I will have to push round in the pram to get them to go down.

Each household is so different, and part of the thrill of a new job was sussing out the lie of the land so I could support the mother.

New mothers all have something in common though, aside from exhaustion: they are all sensitive. With so many hormones raging around their bodies, it's little wonder. That's why I made sure never to take over or appear to be telling them what to do. What's worse than an interfering nanny in the house telling you what you're doing is wrong? I should find myself out of favour rather quickly.

If a mother is floundering with changing a nappy or can't get baby to take the bottle, I would never say, 'Don't do that,' rather, 'Have you tried doing it this way?'

Eye contact, gentle encouragement, smiles, rest and support are all that's needed to get a new mother up on her feet.

Soon Mrs Gordon and her twins were flourishing and we had a lovely little routine in place. The colour was coming back into her cheeks and even Mr Gordon seemed relaxed when he returned home from the hospital to find a steaming-hot home-cooked meal waiting in the dining room.

The way to a new mother's heart might be through gentle support and sleep, but the way to a new father's heart is definitely through home-cooked puddings. Steamed suet pudding with apple and custard usually hits the spot, but from my experience spotted dick or bread and butter pudding work just as well.

I quickly realised Mr Gordon was like all men, my father and brothers included. Place a bowl of something hot, stodgy and sticky and smothered with custard in front of him and he'd stay quiet and content for hours.

'Damn fine pudding this, Nurse Brenda,' he'd sigh happily, scraping up the last bit of custard from the plate.

'Eat up, eat up,' I grinned. 'New fathers need their strength too.'

It was shaping up to be a very nice, happy household indeed.

I'd only been there a few weeks when I took the twins out to the gardens in the square for some fresh air so that Mrs Gordon could get her afternoon nap. Sitting on a bench I got chatting to a fellow nanny.

When I'd joined her she'd been staring into the middle distance with her eyes glazed instead of watching the two young children in her care. A 'park nurse', Miss Whitehead would have called her. Untrained and undisciplined.

'Don't you mind not having a social life?' she grumbled with a sour face. 'It's Saturday night tonight and I'm stuck in again. I never get out in the evening.'

'I don't mind really,' I replied, tucking the blanket up under the twins' chubby little faces.

I often saw nannies huddled together chatting, possibly trading secrets, but I preferred to keep myself to myself and watch over and interact with my charges instead. I was quite certain Miss Whitehead had long since retired and would no longer be pedalling the streets of Kensington spying on errant nannies, but still, I had to make a good impression and one couldn't do that by sitting gossiping.

As I parted from the disgruntled nanny and pounded the streets of Kensington, the children fast asleep in their pram, I thought about it.

Did I mind not having much of a life of my own? Did I mind spending this evening, Saturday night, like every other night? In bed, on my own, with only two babies to keep me company.

I thought long and hard. Honestly, no. This need inside me to create a perfect home life for others was so strong it was all-consuming. I just wanted to replicate my happy home life in as many places as I possibly could. The enjoyment and satisfaction I got from my work far outweighed my need to go and socialise. So far I had received more love from little babies than I had during my own, somewhat disastrous encounters with men.

But as I was busy building a home full of love and stability in Kensington, dark storm clouds were building over-head. Unbeknownst to me, twenty miles away in Surrey, my own home was about to be torn apart. All that I cherished and held dear was destroyed in one single, devastating moment.

The call came just after I'd put the twins down to sleep and a short while after Mr and Mrs Gordon had left for a dinner party. I was looking forward to catching up with some correspondence, but the ringing phone distracted me.

'Gordon residence,' I sang.

'Brenda Ashford?' came the unfamiliar and serious voice.

'Yes, this is she,' I said quietly, a sinking feeling creeping over me.

'I'm calling from Kingston Hospital in Surrey. I'm afraid to say your mother, father and sister have been in a car accident.'

I froze and gripped the hall table for support. 'A . . . are they OK?' I stuttered.

'We need you to come in immediately.'

'Are they OK?' I begged, my voice rising.

'Please come in and speak to the doctor immediately,' replied the woman.

The phone slipped from my hand and in a daze I replaced the handset in the cradle.

This could not be happening. This simply could not be happening.

The phone rang again and I grabbed it. Perhaps it was the nurse again? Ringing to tell me it was all just an awful, dreadful mix-up.

I would have done anything to turn the clock back just five minutes.

'Nurse Brenda?' said Mr Gordon's voice. 'Is everything OK?'

Why he chose to ring remains a mystery to this day. Perhaps he had a hunch all was not well.

'Not really,' I whispered. 'I've just been notified that my parents have been in a car crash.'

'I'm on my way home now,' he said calmly.

I stood rooted to the spot until he and Mrs Gordon burst through the door.

Gently he put a coat around my shoulders and, still wearing his dinner suit, led me to his car outside.

'The twins . . . ?' I said, snapping out of my daze.

'Will be OK,' he said firmly. 'They're with Mrs Gordon.'

I stared out of the window in a trance and watched the rain-splattered streets of London speed past in a blur of neon light. Everywhere people went about their business.

Elvis Presley's first film, *Love Me Tender,* had just opened and queues of giggling girls stretched down the street. Courting couples ran shrieking with laughter to shelter from the rain; friends drank and chattered in bars. London was alive and throbbing.

My world was turning on its axis and with every mile fear clutched my heart. I just knew nothing would ever be the same again.

At the hospital Mr Gordon made an imposing sight as he strode down the corridors in his dinner suit. The hospital was his world, a place where he felt confident and in charge.

'Dr Gordon, consultant obstetrician and gynaecologist,' he boomed when we reached the reception desk. 'I demand to see a doctor.'

Saturday nights were obviously a busy time at Kingston A&E and the receptionist didn't take kindly to being bossed about.

'Take a seat,' she snapped.

'No,' he said, irritation rising in his voice. 'This lady's parents have been in a car crash and we need to see a doctor immediately.'

She slunk off and two minutes later returned with a doctor.

'Please, follow me.' The doctor beckoned gently to a side room.

And with that my heart sank. I knew without him telling me. I would go into that room and things would never be the same again. I wanted to run screaming from the hospital.

Instead I felt Mr Gordon's arm on my shoulder, guiding me to my fate.

'I'm afraid to say the car accident was serious,' the doctor said gently. 'Your mother didn't survive and your father is terribly ill. We don't know yet whether he will pull through. Your sister Kathleen was also in the car and has also sustained injuries.'

I opened my mouth to say something but nothing came out. Suddenly I felt quite small, and all alone in the world.

'I want to see my father,' I squeaked. 'I need to be with him.'

'Of course,' said the doctor.

The room was filled with the sound of scraping chairs and my body seemed to move of its own accord. As we walked I could hear a strange voice and muffled sobs, and realised in surprise they were my own. The tears were still streaming down my face when we reached Father's room.

Father lay as still as stone in his bed. He had a tracheotomy tube in his neck so he could breathe and his face had a sickly grey pallor about it. Wires snaked over his body, pumping oxygen into him.

The blood in my veins turned to ice. 'Oh no . . .' I choked. 'No . . . no . . . no.'

There was an awful stillness in the room that turned my heart over. Just the beeping of machines. I clutched his cold hand in mine and cried until I thought my heart might break.

Mother was gone and my father was fighting for his life. Already I felt the loss of my mother to the bottom of my soul.

A mother is the linchpin, the heart and soul of a family, and now ours had been ripped out. She had only been sixty-eight. Far too young to die.

Who would I confide my hopes and fears in over a cup of tea in the kitchen? Trade stories with or seek advice, wisdom, comfort . . . or simply a slice of cake and a cuddle?

Mother was a permanent fixture in our home, as central to the house as a stove is to a kitchen.

I thought she would be there always. Suddenly it hit me like a thunderbolt. I had never gone home to find my mother not there, stirring something on the stove or smiling at something my father said as she knitted while listening to the wireless, or her soft voice drifting out over the fields calling my siblings and me to come in for supper. She was never not there . . . until now. She would never be there again.

Her loss was simply unimaginable and unspeakably horrific. Not just to me but to every member of my family.

Little did I know it then, but the tragic events of that day were to shape my life in ways I couldn't yet imagine.

Eventually the doctor pulled me to one side.

'Your father is very weak. He has broken every single one of his ribs and lost a lot of blood. It's imperative when he regains consciousness that you don't tell him of your mother's death. That could push him over the edge.'

I nodded dumbly.

Next I visited Kathleen. She was conscious and wearing an eye-patch over her right eye.

'They think I'll lose my sight,' she whispered.

'Oh Kathleen,' I sobbed, hugging her. 'What happened?'

Her voice was barely above a whisper.

'We were driving up to some traffic lights and father was slowing down when suddenly there was an almighty smash. The lorry in front had turned his lights off and Father didn't see him until too late.'

I choked back a sob.

Please, God. Don't let Mother have suffered.

Eventually Mr Gordon drove me home to Kensington. I didn't sleep a wink that night. Just kept turning the awful events of the evening over and over in my mind.

Thoughts whirled round my shattered brain at break-neck speed. But they always came back to the same dilemma. What should I tell Father?

The next day I visited the minister of a local Baptist church and confided in him.

I drew strength from the quietness and stillness of the darkened church. The minister said nothing as I shared the whole story.

'Please, Minister, what do I do?' I sobbed. 'I've been brought up to never tell a lie. How can I lie to my father?'

He paused, then gently took my hands in his. 'Just tell him that she's happy now,' he said softly.

The next two weeks passed in an exhausted blur. The

Gordons were beyond magnificent and Mr Gordon in particular so kind.

'I'm so worried I'm neglecting the twins,' I fretted every time he drove me to the hospital.

'Please don't worry about us,' he said.

On one visit the doctor pulled me aside.

'Your father has regained consciousness and it would appear he is on the mend, but remember what I told you. This is a vital time in his recovery.'

My heart sank and the minister's words rang in my ears. *Just tell him that she's happy now.*

Father managed a weak smile when I walked in to see him.

'Oh Father,' I cried, rushing to his side. 'You gave us quite a fright you know.'

His tracheotomy tube had been removed, but he struggled to speak. He fixed his kind blue eyes on mine and gave me a look so bewildered it broke my heart. Slowly, his frail hand crept across the hospital sheets and he laced his fingers through mine. Gulping, I squeezed them gently.

Stay strong, Brenda. Stay strong.

Father's mouth was as dry as parchment paper and his first word when it came was rasping and barely above a whisper.

'Mother?' he croaked.

I closed my eyes and summoned every ounce of my willpower.

I smiled. 'Mother is happy now,' I said softly.

A light went out in his eyes. He pulled his hand from mine and leaned back heavily against the pillow.

I squeezed back a tear. *He knows.*

Weeks later Father was to recall that he knew she was gone the instant he came round and in many ways I wasn't surprised.

'You sense these things,' he confided in me.

They had been married for thirty-eight years and in all that time had never spent a day apart. They thought the same, felt the same. In many ways they were the same person, their souls so tightly entwined after years of love and companionship.

A fierce love like that burned so brightly. It was almost inconceivable to have one without the other.

None of us children dared voice our fears, but we all felt it the day we buried Mother.

How would we all breathe without her?

At the crematorium we all stared dumbfounded at Mother's coffin. As it started to slide towards the red velvet curtains and disappear, I closed my eyes.

I didn't want to remember Mother in a coffin vanishing behind a set of curtains. I wanted to remember her for the kind, vibrant, loving woman she was.

With my eyes closed I could picture her clearly. With her knitting on her lap, her family gathered around her, humming along to Henry Hall on the wireless. Or laughing as Father made her close her eyes.

'For you, Bobby,' he'd laugh, as he popped a bag of sugared almonds in her hand and planted a gentle kiss on her cheek.

I conjured up that wonderful afternoon we'd had when, as a treat for being accepted into the Norland, Mother had taken me to London to buy some smart shoes and had even bought me an ice-cream sundae at a fancy tea shop.

Hadn't I felt grand sitting in such a smart establishment, where the waitresses wore black and white uniforms, each table was covered with a linen tablecloth, and an orchestra of men wearing tuxedos had serenaded us? I'll never forget the look of pride that shone in Mother's eyes as she delicately sipped her tea. What a memory to cherish always.

But most of all I remember the sweet sensation of her kisses, the softest down on her cheek that would tickle as it brushed against mine.

I touched my cheek as if trying to bring the memory to life.

'I love you, Mother, and I always will,' I whispered.

When I opened my eyes the coffin had gone. My brothers sat lined up, eyes downcast. But Kathleen . . . Kathleen seemed almost to have shrunk into herself. I knew a little of her soul had died too, but looking at her now I saw she was eaten up with a pain so dark and vicious she seemed almost destroyed. Perhaps Mother's death was the catalyst for the terrible events that were to engulf her in later life?

When something as awful as that happens you wonder how life will ever return to normal, but somehow it does.

Poor Bambi, Mother's dog, who was also in the car, had to be put down as he never recovered from his injuries. In some ways it was a small comfort. Mother would at least have her beloved dog by her side.

Father and Kathleen recovered from their injuries. Kathleen regained the sight in her damaged eye and went back to delivering babies, but from that day on she never spoke a word about the accident. She pretended it was the concussion, but I knew she remembered everything. I never pushed her, though. The trauma of that fateful day had affected her in ways I would never know.

Kathleen and I made a pact to take it in turns to spend weekends with Father back at the bungalow he and Mother had shared in Surrey. Slowly but surely I finally got to know my sister a little better. It was tragic and ironic that it took Mother's death to make it happen. I had always known that she and I were different. Even as children I had been bouncy and boisterous, content to get muddy and run wild in the fields. Kathleen was studious, reserved and a little more complicated, as, I suppose, deep thinkers often are.

As we tended to Father together I glimpsed another side to my sister.

'I shall wear black in mourning all year,' she muttered darkly.

This seemed a little excessive to me. As a nanny I obviously couldn't do that, even if I had wanted.

'Isn't that a little, well, over the top, Kathleen?' I ventured. 'I know Mother has gone and we are all grieving, but I do know she wouldn't want our lives to stop.'

'How can I be happy ever again?' she snapped, in a voice so sharp and laden with pain it took my breath away.

After the funeral my time with the Gordons came to an end too.

'I will never forget your kindness in my time of need,' I told them as I packed my bags.

'We should be thanking you, Nurse Brenda,' replied Mr Gordon, a little less gruffly than usual. 'You have been the most wonderful help.'

I left Kensington an older, sadder woman than I had arrived. But the mission I was on burned brightly, perhaps even move so than before. As I pattered down the white mansion steps I had an epiphany so strong it stopped me in my tracks. I put down my bag and umbrella and paused. A soft breeze kissed my cheek and I smiled. My brain hummed with a quiet intensity.

What was my mother's biggest passion, beside my father?

Children and family life.

'Of course,' I murmured, shaking my head. 'Of course.'

Childcare had always been my calling, but now it looked as if it might be my salvation too!

More than anything in the world, Mother had always wanted to be a nanny, but thanks to the restrictive thinking of the time it wasn't deemed a suitable job for a genteel young lady. She had never realised her dream, but thanks to her love and encouragement I had.

My own home life had had the heart ripped out of it, but I owed it to Mother to carry on as before. No – stronger, more dedicated and more determined than before.

I owed it to her to make as many families as happy and content as I could. To restore family harmony and peace to homes the length and breadth of Britain, whatever the price, whatever the cost. Whatever the sacrifice to my own personal happiness, I would do it. Even if it meant never standing still, travelling hundreds of miles and never really unpacking and putting down roots, I would do it. I would do it for Mother to repay her for her unshakeable belief in me.

After all, had it not been for her love and wisdom where would I be now? No, I couldn't crumble. I had to remain strong.

I was no longer just a nanny. I was a woman on a mission. In life I believe we are guided by fate, our own destiny shaped by mysterious, unexplainable forces. Mother's untimely death was in many ways a turning point for me. I knew finally that I would never marry or have children to call my own.

Once parted from such a dream it was surprisingly easy to come to terms with it. From what I could see it wasn't easy to meet a truly good man anyway. The only man I had ever met for whom I really felt strongly was now promised to Jesus. Bill had made every other man seem just ordinary.

Up until that point I could so easily have settled for second best and started my own family, and in doing so I could have turned my back on nannying for ever. Or I could have allowed my grief to swallow me whole, as Kathleen had done.

But life had a different plan for me and for the first time in years I began to see clearly. Mother's spirit could and would live on through my work.

With that I picked up my bag and walked slowly down the steps, through quiet and leafy Courtfield Gardens, and hailed a taxi to my new life.

Testimonial

Nurse Brenda has been with us for five weeks in charge of our twin girls, she has been a wonderful help in every way and we are very sad she's leaving. Her very high professional skill has been coupled with a great ability to fit in with the ordinary day to day life of the family. It is with a great sense of regret that she's leaving.

Mr Gordon

NANNY'S WISDOM

Dealing with grief
After my mother's death it would have been all too easy to go back to bed, turn off the lights and shut out the world. Grief is an awful black hole that can consume you whole. Set yourself little tasks and keep yourself busy and be proud of yourself for getting through each day. Caring for children certainly kept me occupied and stopped me dwelling on my pain, but Mother was never very far from my thoughts and that's fine too. Carry the love you have for a lost one in your heart always and draw strength from it. I always remember the feeling of Mother's downy face when she kissed me. That memory is so vivid in my mind and in a strange way brings me peace whenever I think of it. I may have lost my mother but I haven't lost her love. Above all, be kind to yourself and in time your shattered heart will start to heal.

The way to a man's heart . . .
I have never had much luck with the opposite sex but they say the way to a man's heart is through his stomach. From my experience, all men love puddings, the stickier and sweeter the better. Try this one for spotted dick. Serve steaming hot and smothered in warm custard and watch him melt.

1½ oz (50 g) butter
12 oz (350 g) plain flour
3 tsp baking powder

4½ oz (140 g) shredded suet
3 oz (85 g) caster sugar
3½ oz (115 g) currants
finely grated zest and juice of 2 lemons
3 fl. oz (75 ml) milk
3 fl. oz (75 ml) whipping cream
custard or clotted cream, to serve

Soften half the butter and use to grease a 2½ pint (1.4 litre) pudding basin. Combine the flour, baking powder, suet, sugar and currants in a large bowl, mixing well. Melt the remaining butter and stir into the flour mixture. Stir in the lemon juice and zest. Combine the milk and cream. Slowly stir enough into the mixture to bring it to a dropping consistency. Pour the mixture into the pudding basin. Cover with a double layer of greaseproof paper and tie in place with string. Place the basin in a steamer basket set over boiling water. Cover and steam for about 1–1½ hours until cooked.

Inexpensive fun for children
You don't need expensive toys to keep children entertained. Simply keep a box of odds and ends. You can keep anything in it for children to play with, from old pinecones to seashells, crayons to stickers, balls of wool to postcards, stamps, dice and plastic cutlery. Everytime you go on holiday or to somewhere new, find something to bring home, be it a shell from the beach or a pretty leaf, and add it to your treasure chest. It will always remind you of fun times.

Or if the weather's fine, then get outside into the great outdoors. Children will love doing any of the following: damming streams, having piggyback races, searching for bugs, racing snails, playing hide and seek in a wood, making a mud pie, skimming stones, climbing a tree, hunting for frogspawn, picking fruit straight from the bush, playing conkers, running through leaves, burying an adult in the snow or sand, jumping in muddy puddles, rolling down a hill, searching for monsters, playing soccer in a field, collecting leaves and flowers, paddling in streams with a net or dancing in the rain. Best of all? They are all absolutely free. Father took us to a smart Italian restaurant called Frascatti's once a year as a treat and I always enjoyed it, but to be honest, I enjoyed it much more when we all played make-believe games in the fresh air.

5

Troubleshooting Nanny

Horsey, horsey, don't you stop
Let your feet go clippety clop,
So when your tail goes swish
And your wheels go round,
Giddy up, we're homeward bound.
Children's song by Roberts,
Box, Cox and Butler (1938)

Whilst I was gathering every ounce of my reserve, Britain rose from the ashes. The late 1950s were golden years, brought about by full employment, and people finally began to forget the austerity they'd lived with for so long.

'You will see a state of prosperity such as we have never had in my lifetime – nor indeed in the history of this country,' said the then prime minister Harold Macmillan in July 1957. 'Indeed let us be frank about it – most of our people have never had it so good.'

In my darkest hours I didn't felt lucky. I felt consumed with grief. I missed Mother so much it was like a physical pain in my chest.

But my siblings and I kept our pain hidden, for Father's sake.

I went about my business in my own quiet way, my pledge to fulfil Mother's long-held dreams driving me on. Travelling from home to home, Scotland to Essex, Hampstead to Chelsea, Surrey to Hampshire. Rarely staying longer than three months but usually just a few weeks. Just enough time to get the mother on her feet and a good routine established.

Then my feet would grow itchy and I would become restless. Many of the mothers offered me permanent positions in their home, but I had no interest in putting down roots. I just wanted to help transform the house and make it as happy and settled as I possibly could, then pack my bags and be on my way.

In many ways it was an extraordinary existence. In just a matter of weeks I threw every ounce of devotion, patience and energy I had into a household. There was always so much to do upon arrival at a new house. Settling the mother and ensuring she returned to full health after the birth, getting up every four hours in the night to feed the baby, establishing a routine, helping to make the baby's older siblings feel included and loved, and making sure the new father didn't feel left out and was a valued cog in the wheel.

For one so tiny, a new baby can certainly make an enormous impact on a family unit and every minute of my time would be spent smoothing, easing, unruffling, calming, coaxing, encouraging, cajoling and gently guiding the family into their new positions. But it was still always a surprise to hear the mother's protestations when I packed my bags to leave.

'Please don't go, Nanny,' cried one woman. 'You've gained my children's confidence . . .' 'But you're part of our family now,' tried to reason another. 'You're invaluable,' was another one I heard a lot.

But I didn't want to be invaluable to just one family. By staying put how could I possibly honour Mother's memory?

Months turned to years, but still my energy never waned. Many more houses to help, I told myself.

Did I miss not having a home to call my own? Not being able to settle in one place? Get to know the area, the community, make permanent friendships or even establish myself within the local church community? Perhaps a little. But the stronger urge within me, to help as many mothers as I could, drove me on.

Was I running from my pain? Keeping myself busy to ignore the dull ache left by Mother's absence? Maybe I was, but I also owed it to her memory to keep going, to replicate the home life she had given me the length and breadth of Britain.

'But you're Norland-trained,' one nanny gasped when we got chatting in the park. 'Why don't you work for royalty or diplomats?'

'I don't give two hoots for that kind of world,' I replied smoothly. 'I'd rather stay here on British soil.'

In 1958 I realised I had been troubleshooting for two years and was well on my way to paying back my bursary to the Norland. I had travelled many miles, yet still the road felt less travelled to me. I was exhausted from waking every three to four hours the majority of the time, but a long way from being burnt out. Although I was approaching forty and laughter lines had etched into my face, I still felt full of stamina and open to learning. And what rich experiences!

With every home I passed through I learned something new about the complicated job of caring for little folk and creating balance within a home. Keep the mother happy and the home will always have harmony. Listen, really listen, to a child by getting down to his or her level. As for the babies? Keep them to a four-hourly feeding routine and lavish them with plenty of cuddles and they should flourish too. It's not so complicated after all.

The arrival of a baby into a family unit is a momentous occasion and for siblings not always a happy one. All children bar none experience jealousy driven by their extreme love for their mother when a new baby arrives on the scene.

'I can't stop him clinging to me when I'm feeding the baby,' wailed one desperate mother about her three-year-old.

'Gentle persuasion,' I replied calmly. 'Your older child will need a lot more attention in these coming weeks than your baby, believe it or not.' And with that I got down on my hands and knees to talk to the put-out toddler.

'I see you've been having a tea party with your teddy,' I grinned. 'Who else is coming to tea?'

The toddler's face lit up. 'Well, mummy teddy and daddy teddy too.'

'Oh how marvellous,' I cried, clapping my hands.

Tantrum diverted, we had a perfectly lovely game after that. Children love to be with adults who understand play at their level. It doesn't have to be a teddies' tea party. It could be pretending a cardboard box is a train and going on a marvellous adventure, painting a picture or simply reading a book.

The more attention and love you lavish on that child the less he or she will feel isolated from the new family unit. But if diversion tactics didn't work, I would try to get the older child involved instead of clinging to his or her poor mother's knee.

'Why don't you help Mummy feed the baby their bottle?' I would say, helping him or her to feed the baby. 'Aren't you doing wonderfully, you clever thing.'

Soon all jealousy would be forgotten by the aggrieved child, who would be basking in the glow of praise.

I passionately believe there is no problem that can't be solved by immersing yourself in a child's world. Get down to the children's level, see the world through their eyes.

This works particularly well, in my opinion, with children prone to tantrums. We've all been there and seen the red mist that always descends before a good old wobbler.

Often tantrums can be avoided by changing the way we speak to our children. Don't just say no without offering an explanation. Intelligent children will always need to know why they can't have more sweets, go on the highest slide or not run when they should walk. Don't automatically say no, talk it through instead. If no really does mean no, then try not to use the word all the time. You'd be surprised how many times the word no is said to a small child.

Instead of saying 'No, you can't watch television,' just think about it and then rephrase it. 'Yes, when you've tidied up your toys.' Instead of 'No, you can't go and play with your friend,' suggest that 'Yes, of course you can, but at the weekend so you have something to look forward to.'

If that doesn't work and a full-blown wobbler develops, never, ever raise your voice. You will have lost control if you do that. My mother never shouted at me and I hope I have never shouted at a child in my care. Instead, remember to breathe deeply, count to ten and give your child a cuddle. If the tantrum continues, then explain that such behaviour will not be tolerated and he or she will be removed.

If the screaming continues then the child must be taken to his or her room. Not a naughty step, where the child will continue to be seen and heard, which is surely exactly what he or she desires, but out of sight and earshot, until the child has calmed down enough to return to the room and be rewarded with a hug.

One thing I will simply never tolerate is bad manners, fussy eaters and untidiness. If you can't get a child to put away all the toys completely at the end of the day, at least get him or her to tidy up.

'A place for everything and everything in its place,' I always say. And lead by example. 'Always hang your things up when you come in. The floor is the untidy child's table.'

In the late 1950s, when rationing had all but died out, I started to see many mothers indulge fussy eaters and start giving them options. This is a mistake in my book. Maybe it was the result of my public show-down with Miss Whitehead when she insisted I eat all the beetroot on my plate, but I took a hard line on fussy eating. 'This is a home, not a restaurant, and you will jolly well try it before you turn your nose up at it,' I would say. Children shouldn't take for granted having a well-stocked larder and fridge.

By the late 1950s, when there was more access to exotic imported ingredients, Mediterranean food was all the rage, but when I had to cook I stuck to the good old-fashioned foods of my childhood like pies, puddings and roasts.

It was a brave child who turned up his or her nose at Nanny's cottage pie! So many children and adults lived on relatively little throughout the war, and they certainly didn't have the luxury of choice, but everyone got by and no one starved. Be grateful for the food on your plate, for you are lucky it is there at all.

Maybe I sound old-fashioned, but sticking hard and consistently to these principles has always improved the behaviour of children in my care and in a short space of time too.

The most important thing I think I learned from the Norland, and which I hope I brought to every home I passed through, was to encourage the mother to spend time playing with her child.

A child needs love and attention. Even if it's a thirty-minute game once in a day, every child just wants to spend time with his or her mummy, basking in her attention. I do wish parents would put down their mobile phones and laptops and make their children the sole recipients of their time and love for part of their day. Some mothers, of course, were simply too tired or busy and had forgotten how to play with their children. I wouldn't tell them what I was doing, but I was secretly showing them how to play.

Every day I read to the children in my care. Reading creates such a lovely routine and helps a young mind to blossom. Or we'd let our imaginations run wild. Any old box can be a pirate ship, or a sheet draped over two chairs a secret den.

Let them create secret worlds. Give them your undivided attention, laugh and join in and they will love you for it. Their childhood will last that much longer too.

After so many years in other women's homes it was inevitable that I would come across a mother who would resent me. But I like to think it was just the one.

Mrs Lillian Schaffer and her husband Neil were wealthy and lived in a large open-plan house in North London with all the latest mod cons, including a fridge and a washing machine.

When I arrived it took me all of two minutes to realise that their eldest child, Jennifer, had a ferocious temper and was horribly spoilt.

'Take her off somewhere and give her sweets,' snapped Lillian to her husband. 'She has been screaming so loudly all day I can't hear myself think.'

Jennifer was dragged kicking and screaming to her bedroom.

'She's a terribly behaved kid,' she sighed to me. 'I don't know how I'm going to cope when this one arrives.' With that she placed a hand on her large bump. 'She'll just have to get used to it I suppose.'

Annoyance bristled inside me. Kids are baby goats. Jennifer was a child. It showed such a lack of respect. I didn't have a terribly good feeling about this appointment.

Suddenly we both became aware of a commotion overhead.

I stared up at a large mezzanine balcony and my jaw dropped to the ground.

A door had flown open and there was Mr Schaffer strid-ing stark-naked along the corridor without a care in the world . . . and I had a bird's-eye view.

'Oh gracious,' I said, averting my gaze.

That was the first time I'd seen a man's appendage and it wasn't a pretty sight.

A second later he was in the bathroom and the sound of the shower went on.

I looked flabbergasted at Mrs Schaffer, but she didn't raise so much as an eyebrow. I could see this was going to be a most peculiar house to work in.

A few days later Mrs Schaffer was taken into hospital to give birth and I was left alone with the stripping husband and their truculent child.

Jennifer was like most naughty children. She needed discipline and more love; not the hearty slap Mr Schaffer would have me issue. With some gentle coax-ing and firm encouragement I had soon engaged her and gradually she began eating all her tea and playing a little better.

One night I had just retired to bed when Mr Schaffer burst into my room. I pulled the sheets up around me, quite alarmed, but he plonked himself down on the end of my bed like it was the most normal thing in the world.

'I've just got back from the hospital,' he said. 'My wife's not very happy with you.'

'But why?' I gasped.

He smirked. 'I told her how well behaved Jennifer's being now that you're here.'

Oh thank you very much.

That was quite sure to enrage her. Sure enough, when she returned she was very frosty towards me and when my two weeks came to an end I was most relieved to go.

With each passing job I quickly realised, though, that with the exception of Mr Schaffer's blasé attitude towards nudity, very little shocked me.

By the late 1950s the wealthy women I worked for had luxuries I could only have dreamed of. So many labour- and time-saving appliances were made more widely available in the 1950s – the decade of domesticity. Washing machines, electric stoves, toasters, kettles, vacuum cleaners and oh glory of glories, the electric iron. No more wrestling with a hot flat iron that needed heating over an open stove.

I thought back to my training at Pembridge Square and how I and all the girls in my set had sweated and toiled on laundry days. As I watched a mother glide her new steam iron over her husband's shirts, pressing them in a jiffy, I could only shake my head in amazement. If only she knew.

I always bit my tongue, of course. No one likes to hear someone harp on about what it was like in their day, but there were occasions when one found it hard to resist. Especially when I heard a new mother grumbling about changing her child's nappy. Now that disposable nappies were so readily available, women were free from the back-breaking task of scrubbing countless soiled terry-cloth ones.

'You should have seen the ones we had to wash when I was training,' I'd chuckle when I saw a young mother wrinkling her nose in disgust. 'At least you can just throw them in the bin.'

In many ways women didn't realise how good they had it now. They had freedom and choices.

Some called it the greatest scientific invention of the twentieth century. I don't know about that, but there is no doubting the pill changed the lives of women for ever once it became widely available from 1961. Suddenly women could have their cake and eat it too. They weren't confined to the home and raising an ever-expanding family. They could choose to start their families later and pursue further education and a career on their own terms. Slowly I also began to realise that many of the women I worked for were leaving the nursery to go back to work or start interesting new careers.

Ordinary women were inspired by the highly publicised feats of some extraordinary women. In the 1950s Jacqueline Cochran, an American pilot, was the first woman to break the sound barrier, and Ann Davison became the first woman to sail single-handed across the Atlantic.

I saw mothers fly planes, run businesses, begin exacting jobs or even, in one case, have a planned caesarean so she could go off on a fortnight's skiing holiday leaving her baby with me. They were liberated in a way my mother's generation could never have dreamed of.

My father witnessed all this too, but increasingly the modern world just washed over him. I visited him as often as I could but more and more often I found him sitting sadly on his own. It was as though he was just going through the motions, moving about as if in a dream world. As we had feared, he never recovered from Mother's death. He still went to his office as often as he could, but even there he couldn't escape Mother's memory.

'You won't believe what his secretary told him,' hissed Kathleen, still in black, when I visited her one afternoon. Kathleen looked terribly upset and whatever it was had clearly rattled her.

'She told him that she was a clairvoyant and she'd been contacted by Mother with a message she simply had to pass on.'

'What on earth?' I blustered.

'Yes, apparently she said that Father's not to worry about the silver thimble. She has one now.'

I stood silently as I allowed her words to sink in. We knew that sometime ago Father had had a terrible job finding Mother a silver thimble that she had wanted.

'Does he believe it?' I asked.

'Yes, I think so,' she fumed. 'I mean it's outrageous saying things like that to a widowed man. It's not natural to dabble in things like that.'

I didn't know what to make of it, but it left me with a strange feeling in my tummy.

Soon after, and exactly two years after Mother's death, I was working for a family in Micheldever in Hampshire. It was slightly strange, as the man of the house had a hook instead of a hand. I never asked why; it would have felt most impolite. He and his wife were lovely, though, and had two beautiful children and a new baby. The hook did nothing to curtail his life and he managed to drive, dress himself, go to work and cradle the baby with his good hand.

The call came one Sunday morning. I was due to drive over and see Father and Kathleen later that day. A nagging feeling of unease had stalked me all day. Had Father really received a message from beyond the grave? Was he to believe a so-called message from Mother about a silver thimble?

When Kathleen called I knew what she was going to say before the words were even out of her mouth.

'I have to tell you,' she said quietly. 'Father's died.'

'I know,' I said simply.

'How do you know?' she gasped.

'I don't know, I just do,' I replied.

Funny how in our society death is much feared, discussed and obsessed over, but in my father's case everything continued just as before. Time didn't stand still.

By the time I reached his bungalow, Kathleen, ever the professional nurse, had called everybody and the funeral parlour had even come and collected Father's body to take him to the local mortuary. She was so organised and efficient. There was nothing left to do except sit and talk.

'What happened?' I asked.

'Father went out to mow the lawn after lunch,' she said in a halting voice. 'The first I realised that something was wrong was when I saw the lawnmower go past the window on its own. I rushed outside and found him dead on the ground. Too early to tell yet, but a suspected heart attack,' she went on. 'It would have been quick.'

We sat in silence as I digested the information. Father had been seventy and had lasted twenty-four months without his beloved wife.

The kitchen clock ticked, next door's cat strolled across Father's half-mowed lawn, the kettle came to the boil for the cup of tea Father liked after gardening.

I could feel pain clawing my heart – first Mother, now Father – but I suppressed it.

'Well,' I sighed. 'It was a glorious death.'

Kathleen nodded her agreement.

I didn't mean to sound flippant. My father had avoided being blown up, shot or going insane in the trenches during the First World War, and had served his country again through countless enemy raids during the Second World War. A peaceful and mercifully quick death amongst his beloved roses was the best he could have hoped for.

'He's with Mother now,' said Kathleen softly. 'The reunion he had been dreaming of.'

I nodded. 'Bet they're both up there now.' I smiled sadly. 'Mother knitting a baby's bonnet, Father sipping a stout, Henry Hall playing in the background.'

Suddenly I realised, and one by one the hairs on the back of my neck stood up. Father had died on a Sunday afternoon – Mother and Father's hallowed time together! They had always insisted on having Sunday afternoons on their own together, with us children sent out to play. Even when they were caring for evacuees during the war nothing had interrupted this tradition.

Father had gone to join Mother during 'their time'. Now they would be together for eternity.

Testimonial

During the short period that Nurse Ashford has been with us the improvement in the behaviour of our elder daughter has been noticeable. She has a way of gaining children's confidence. Nurse Ashford has also devoted her whole time, patience and energy into the welfare of the baby.

Mr Schaffer

NANNY'S WISDOM

Keep a harmonious home

I know it's hard in this fast-paced, frantic, modern world, but I do wish people would try harder not to let stress and anger into the home. If families treated their homes as a sanctuary, then the people in it would remain calmer. I could never believe it when I heard people bickering in front of their children. Why oh why would parents subject them to that? Children learn so much from their parents, so when they hear arguing it normalises it and teaches them that shouting is perfectly acceptable behaviour. It is just so damaging for children. I never heard my own mother and father raise their voices to each other, not once, and as result we respected them. If they said no, we listened and we did what they told us. We grew up knowing the difference between right and wrong.

Newborn routine

All newborns need a routine. The correct equipment supports that routine. As a rule of thumb this is what a newborn requires: 4 nightgowns, 4 vests, 4 matinee jackets (cardigans), nappies, 1 dozen muslin cloths, large shawl, 2 blankets for pram, and as cot covers, 3 pairs of bootees, 2 fitted waterproof sheets, 4 cotton sheets, pram cover, cotton wool, 2 soft towels, nappy rash cream, baby soap, baby hairbrush, nail scissors, baby sponge and a bucket for soiled nappies. Bottle-fed babies also need a steriliser, 6 bottles, brush for cleaning bottles, teats and dried milk.

I aimed to feed baby four-hourly, not on demand. If a baby screamed for food between those feed times I would try to give cool boiled water. Hungrier babies will need three-hourly feeds. To help keep track of feeding times I'd jot them down in a notepad. Newborn babies tend to sleep a lot and I would always encourage that. Daytime naps should be taken wherever possible outside in the fresh air in a cot or pram. I would discourage sleeping past 5 p.m. and always try to keep baby awake with a little kickabout play on a mat. If they are still napping past 5 p.m. they will not go down at 7 p.m.

In many ways newborn babies are very straightforward. They cry if they are hot, cold, hungry, wet or overtired. I would always consider all the possible causes when I had a baby that was crying a lot and not just assume he or she was crying for milk.

I've noticed that a lot of new mothers panic and use milk to try and soothe a crying baby, when most of the time the baby needs a change, a burping, or even just a little walk round the garden. Too much milk can be a bad thing for a baby's tiny tummy.

All children are different, so I always told mothers not to be scared to use their intuition and let the baby guide them. Watch and listen carefully and try to work the baby out. Have a routine in mind, but don't be a slave to it.

Some babies I cared for suffered from dreadful colic and would scream the house down. Unfortunately this usually coincided with the return home from work of Father. If gripe water didn't work, then I would drive baby round in the car, as motion settles colicky babies, or otherwise a dummy helped. I don't really encourage the use of dummies, but babies who suffer with colic or reflux, or a terribly sucky baby, will on occasion need it.

Include new fathers
I do so feel for the new father when a baby comes on the scene. Often he is quite forgotten in the flurry of excitement that a new arrival brings. Everything, quite rightly, is focused on the mother and baby. But when I saw an anxious new father hovering at the nursery door I would welcome him in and try to include him in the duties. Fathers need time and space to bond with their baby, just as much as new mothers do, in fact sometimes more so. A mother can feed and do so much for her baby, but a father can quite often feel like a spare part and if not included can grow resentful. Some of my favourite times were showing new fathers how to change a nappy and seeing the wonder in their eyes when they realised they had done it all by themselves. I do wish people would remember that a father is a vital cog in the wheel and as such every effort should be made to include him.

6

Community Calling

Little Bo-peep has lost her sheep,
And can't tell where to find them;
Leave them alone, and they'll come home,
And bring their tails behind them.

Nineteenth-century
English nursery rhyme

The smart townhouse in an even smarter Hampstead suburb had it all. It soared into the sky like a huge white-iced wedding cake, its glossy black wrought-iron railings a barrier against the outside world.

Its occupants wanted for nothing. The kitchen housed the latest in technological wizardry, from blenders to fridges, irons to washing machines. In the past, fridges and appliances had looked like pieces of industrial machinery, but here everything looked so sleek and new and was all fitted together. One could open the fridge, pull open a sleek drawer to remove a cooking utensil and be back at the oven in a jiffy. And instead of the vast scrubbed oak table that usually dominated most kitchens and copper pans hanging from the ceiling, this one just had endless counter space and drawers. There was a place for everything and everything matched. I'd never seen anything like it.

As Mrs Beasley, the lady of the house, whisked me from room to room showing me where everything was my eyes were out on stalks at the sheer luxury and size of it all.

'What a beautiful home you have,' I murmured, impressed. 'Your boys must love living here.'

'You would think, Nurse Brenda,' she snapped back, irritation flickering over her face. 'We could do with a bigger garden. These townhouses have such dashed small grounds. Its infuriating.'

'What are your neighbours like?' I asked.

She turned to stare at me, a look of utter bemusement on her face. 'Our neighbours?' she said at last, wrinkling her perfect nose. 'Why I have no idea.'

Suddenly, I realised. The idea of knowing her neighbours was so alien to her she had probably never stopped to consider who lived on the other side of the wall. But then, I supposed, her neighbours had probably never stopped to consider her either.

It was so strange, and it only really hit me now as I paused in the grand marble entrance hall of my new home. No one knew his or her neighbours any more. Why now, in 1960, was the sense of community breaking up to the point that people didn't really immerse themselves in their neighbours' lives any more? It was so short-sighted, if you asked me. Befriending the people who live in your community is one of the single most life-enhancing things you can do.

Having a community around you that can be fired into life when the chips are down, or which is simply on hand to help out or there to share a spontaneous cup of tea with, is everything.

Gradually, as I moved from home to home, I'd noticed the houses I worked in getting smarter and more luxurious. The mothers were for the most part lovely ladies who would have done anything for anyone. But their sense of isolation from the rest of the world was increasing as the luxury within grew.

Women didn't stand around doing communal washday any more, not now they had machines in their own homes; no one needed to shop, dawdle and chat at weekly markets when they could whizz round and do all their shopping under one roof in these new supermarkets that one kept hearing so much about. Motor cars and televisions were marvellous, but they just seemed to speed up our lives and distance us ever further from our fellow human beings.

Doors that were once left open were now firmly shut. Washing machines and labour-saving devices were all well and good, but as people strove to increase their material possessions, it occurred to me, what good was it trying to impress the neighbours if one didn't actually know them? I don't mean to sound like a stick-in-the-mud, harping back to a golden age, but to me community and the friendships fostered within are more valuable than gold.

Writing in the *Norland Quarterly*, Dr Josephine Macalister Brew agreed with me:

It is a frightening thing; we are getting so many more labour-saving devices into the home, we are developing a scientific knowledge of how to cook by number instead of by faith as we used to, we are getting to know the relative properties of calories and vitamins, about first aid, physical health and hygiene and yet all of these things will be lost unless we pay equal attention to the things of the emotions, the things of the mind and the things of the spirit.

So many people in these modern labour-saving houses are really just drifting through life; labour saving really means they have more leisure in which to be dissatisfied. It is the *art* of living which so many people have lost which could help to recapture life.

President Roosevelt said this: 'Peace and happiness, indeed the history of the world will depend on two things – education and personal relationships – and personal relationships are very largely a matter of education'. We used to think that if we could not get on with people there was not a thing you could do about it, and a number of people imagine not getting on with others sets them apart as rather distinguished characters – you know – *I am a little more choosy*.

The art of getting on with people is, of course, a duty, but it is also a terrific adventure. Do what you don't like, and you will be surprised at the results, surprised that in learning to grasp life as an adventure it becomes what you think or hope it will be. We can all learn how to get on with people.

Hear, hear, I say. We can and should all learn to get on with people – especially those within our own communities.

Looking back can teach us to look forward. The war years might have been a long, tough slog for so many, but there was no doubting that during that time the sense of camaraderie and community was stronger then than at any other time in living memory.

During the Blitz everyone in the small community of Appleton, where I worked in my first job, pulled together and did their bit. Men and women of all ages and backgrounds manned the Air Raid Protection headquarters, otherwise known as 'the post'. It became a second home to many and laughter and cheery chatter spilled from the post day and night. The Women's Voluntary Service did an excellent job dishing out sausage, chips and fried bread for all those helping out with the war effort.

If the worst happened and Jerry managed to bomb your house, the community would swoop into action and have it fixed in no time. If it was beyond repair, they'd usher bewildered and scared mothers and children into what little room the villagers had left in their own homes.

Even members of the Women's Institute cycled round handing out free jam. Thanks to the war the village had come alive and, to quote Churchill, had found 'its soul'. National pride had imbued our villagers with a strong sense of comradeship. Doors were never closed and you were never really alone. During my three years in Hertfordshire at Redbourn Day Nursery, caring for children whose mothers had gone to work in the factories, I saw it all over again.

Willing grandmothers dropped grandchildren off while the mothers worked; the milkman was a friend to all and regularly topped up the children's milk provisions for free; the midwife was on first-name terms with everyone; and the local boys and evacuees mixed happily as they raced in and out of each other's homes.

The hub of the community had been Redbourn Common, where people converged in one happy mass of humanity to chat, update each other on the latest war news, or simply to watch the local lads and evacuees pit their skills against each other in football matches.

But here in this smart postcode I very much doubted for a second that the lady of the house would be baking cakes for her neighbours. Besides which, she had a cook to do all that for her in her super-smart kitchen . . .

'We have staff, so you won't need to worry about cooking for the boys,' said Mrs Beasley, flicking one perfectly manicured hand in the direction of the kitchen.

'Ah,' she said, as the front door swung open and a rather harassed-looking gentleman, dressed smartly in a Harris tweed coat with velvet collar, strode in. 'My husband's home.'

'Come on, darling,' he said impatiently, tapping his wristwatch. 'We really must get going if we're to make our flight.'

After a flurry of kisses and last-minute checks, the couple departed on holiday, leaving me in sole charge of their two boys, Jeremy, six, and John, four.

It may seem inconceivable now, but back then it was quite the norm for upper-middle-class parents to go on holiday leaving their children in the care of a perfect stranger, albeit a Norland-trained one.

Nowadays you couldn't imagine doing it for a second, but no one batted an eyelid when I was working. 'It's far too difficult to take the boys skiing,' the lady of the house had said before she scurried into the waiting black taxi. Would she have been judged for her actions? Not a bit, and as a professional nanny I wasn't about to judge her either.

Besides, I was used to it. Mothers like her had their freedom, indeed expected it. If she hadn't been off skiing she'd have been playing golf or bridge with her friends. They were accustomed to leading a somewhat more selfish lifestyle than their 1940s counterparts.

I didn't mind; it did, after all, keep me in employment. The only problem with entering a stranger's house was not knowing where anything was.

I turned to Jeremy and John and took in their smart appearances. They wore matching Harris tweed coats with velvet collars, like their father's, and the younger boy even had that ultimate prestige item, a fur-trimmed bonnet.

All the well-to-do children of that time were always dressed impeccably, like mini adults. If they'd been girls their wardrobes would have been groaning with smocked Viyella dresses, white socks, soft leather shoes and little knitted cardigans. I knew without even looking in their nursery that it would be stacked with all the latest toys.

Talk about wealth and privilege. These little boys didn't want for anything. Except, perhaps, manners.

Along with the breakdown of community, I had also seen over the years a certain relaxation in attitudes towards manners and etiquette. During the war and into the 1950s, manners and etiquette were *everything*. Good table manners had been drummed into me growing up and so as far as I was concerned my charges should be brought up with the same respect for etiquette.

We always made sure our hands were washed before we ate, no elbows on the table, you ate as much as you could on your plate, never spoke with your mouth full, enquired politely whether you might be excused from the table after eating and always made sure to say please and thank you.

I firmly believe that if you show respect to others they in turn will show you respect. This includes listening to people when they are talking to you without interrupting them, and looking them in the eye and smiling when you meet them. It never hurts to always try and remember people's names when introduced and to use their name when talking to them.

I love this little poem as there is so much truth in it.

> *Hearts, like doors, will open with ease*
> *To very, very little keys.*
> *And don't forget that two of these,*
> *Are 'Thank you, Sir,' and, 'If you please'.*

Isn't it lovely?

It's the little things in life that count and kindness costs nothing. Manners are part of our national heritage and should be observed keenly. Do unto others as you would have them do unto you. It may sound old-fashioned, but I have lived my life by that principle.

By and large I'd never really seen any cheeky or disrespectful children. Even the evacuee children from the slums of the East End, whose mothers had some of the fruitiest language I've ever heard, always said please and thank you. And if they didn't nod respectfully and remove their caps to me, the midwife, the police or the local doctor, a swift clip round the ear from their mothers would soon remind them to. But now, with this new so-called 'flower power' generation, remembering your p's and q's wasn't so fashionable and manners were in short supply – as was fabric, judging by the length of the skirts I saw on the girls striding past on the streets outside.

Discipline and boundaries seemed to have fallen by the wayside. I blamed the relaxation of standards. Frequently when I joined a new house I took over from an untrained and relaxed au pair, most of whom didn't even speak the language and therefore couldn't discipline a child. Au pairs were all the rage, so it seemed.

Well, this nanny wouldn't stand for it. Not on my watch! If Mother and Father had brought me up to believe anything, it was that manners count.

'Well now, boys,' I smiled. 'I hope we have a marvellous week together. Would you like to show me to your nursery?'

Jeremy, the older boy, stared at me before belligerently poking out his tongue and shoving his little brother as he pushed past him to storm off. Miss Whitehead, who was always such a stickler for good manners, would have had a blue fit at this. Instinct told me not to tell him off too heartily. The poor mite was probably bewildered at his parents going off in such a rush, and wondering just who was this strange woman telling them what to do.

Instead I gently caught him as he pushed past and then crouched down so I was at his height. Throughout my career I have always made an effort to get down to a child's level to talk to him or her. How can you communicate with children or expect them to respect you if you talk down to them?

I looked him in the eye, smiled brightly, and gently cupped his chin in my hand. 'A cheerful spirit gets on quick, a grumbler in the mud will stick, Jeremy.'

He stared at me, baffled. 'You're not going to tell me off or put me on the naughty step?' he asked.

'Whatever for?' I said. 'I'd much rather you were with us.' And then, a shade more firmly: 'But I don't tolerate people poking tongues out or pushing and shoving. In this house we respect one another and do unto others as we would have others do unto us. If you don't, you shall be asked to go to your bedroom, and that would be such a waste of time when we could be doing other things like having fun.'

Do you know, for the rest of the day that's just what we did. We got down on our hands and knees and played trains and jigsaws, and even put on a play about pirates. And when Jeremy did overstep the boundaries and I caught him repeatedly grabbing toys from his little brother, he swiftly found himself in his bedroom.

'It's not fair,' he yelled, his little face growing puce with rage. 'I hate you.'

'That's a shame,' I replied calmly. 'Because I don't hate you. But I am going to send you to your bedroom until you can learn to share. You're not the only pebble on the beach,' I said smoothly, drowning out his outraged yells as I closed the door behind me.

When he emerged sheepishly ten minutes later and said sorry to his little brother, he was rewarded with a hug. 'Well done for saying sorry and calming down,' I smiled. 'You see, it's such a waste of time being beastly. We much prefer it when you're here with us.'

Children are so clever and will interpret things in such unusual ways that it is vitally important that we lead by example if we are to expect them to follow our advice, particularly when it comes to manners and behaviour. I still always remember one Nurse Waters recounting the time she tried to dissuade her young charge Jane from fighting with her brother Charles.

'When disentangling Jane and Charles from a fight, young Jane said hotly, "Well, he hit me first." Thereupon I told her the Christian duty, but was somewhat taken aback a little later to hear anguished screams from Charles and Jane saying triumphantly, "I didn't hit him back, I hit him first." '

The rest of the week passed by in a flash and Jeremy turned out to be quite the most delightful child. He was just highly strung, which usually means intelligent in my opinion.

It's always worth taking the extra time to try to understand exactly what it is that makes a child tick. Watch and quietly observe a child playing. Does he or she hang back or plough straight in there? Is a child loud and rambunctious, or unsure and sensitive?

Children are not peas in a pod; no two are alike. They are rarely what they appear to be on the outside and bad manners are often a mask for something else. The ones who shout, holler and demand things are more often than not seeking attention. Give them your attention in other ways, by playing with them and listening to them. Jeremy wasn't really a badly behaved child. For all his bravado I could tell that deep down he was probably a sensitive child, and intelligent too.

I suppose some parents would have given him a short, sharp smack, but I was a Norland Nanny. By training with them I had rejected the use of smacking and jolly grateful I was for that too.

Imagine if I had left that little boy with a stinging hand mark on his leg? I would have lost his trust for ever, and once lost trust is something you can never get back. In his parents' absence he needed my understanding and respect.

Taking the time to show respect will never fail you and is the single most important thing you can do for a child, in my opinion. In no time at all Jeremy was an absolute poppet, saying please and thank you, and generally doing what was asked of him.

By the time the key turned in the lock and Mr and Mrs Beasley returned from their skiing holiday, I was almost sad to leave.

'Welcome home,' I smiled, standing behind my two charges with my hands resting on their shoulders. I'd made sure their faces had been wiped squeaky clean with a warm flannel and their clothing was neat and tidy. It wouldn't do to have the lady of the house thinking things had gone to pot in her absence.

'Hello, boys,' Mrs Beasley beamed, looking her two sons up and down. 'We have missed you.'

Over afternoon tea the boys filled their mother in on the past week's activities.

'Nurse Brenda and I have had great fun. We put on a pirate show,' piped up Jeremy, before turning to me. 'Can I get down from the table now, please?'

Mr Beasley dropped his newspaper on the table with a thud, his jaw dropping as he stared at his eldest son. Later, as I made to leave, Mrs Beasley paid me my wages and pulled me to one side.

'Well I don't know how you did it, Nurse Brenda,' she whispered. 'Not only has everything gone so smoothly with the boys, but their behaviour has improved dramatically too. I wish I could get them to do that.'

I gave her a wry grin. 'Don't worry. If I've learned anything from working with children it's that they will happily do what a stranger tells them but never what their own mother asks of them.'

'In that case,' she grinned, 'you will return, won't you?'

'I'll try my best, Mrs Beasley,' I said. In truth it was unlikely, as through sheer word of mouth I had found myself booked solid for the two years since my father's death and was now booked solid for the next year ahead as well.

In many ways my busy diary was a blessing, as it meant I'd had little time to dwell on Father's death. Although, strange as it might sound, the grief hadn't sliced quite as deeply as it had with Mother. Perhaps it was because deep inside I knew that they were together now. It had been Father's will. He simply hadn't been able to live without her.

After Mrs Beasley I went from one wealthy home to another. All my bookings were through word of mouth, so I had no need to find work through the Norland any longer. In fact, I quickly began to realise I was what one might now call the 'go-to' nanny for the smart set, as I was passed around a wealthy circle of friends.

The wealthy set were one thing, but I thank my lucky stars I was never a nanny to the rich and famous.

One nurse, Frances Armitage wrote of her time working for a film star in California in the late 1950s.

I am caring for her adopted daughter, aged 3. We live upstairs in the nursery and I have a very modern kitchen where I cook our meals. The washing machine is also one of those modern ones, which does the drying also.

It is a nerve-wracking existence. We never know from one day to the next what to expect. It is quite usual to be told one night at 10 p.m. to pack a few things and catch a plane early next day, for perhaps three or four days. Some days we go to the studio and the little girl has her hair cut by Mummy's hairdresser. It is quite fun meeting the actors and having cups of coffee with them in the studios. The life of an actress seems so hard. They spend days doing scenes which only take a few minutes on screen. What I dislike most about living with film people is the way they keep their children up so late and there is nothing one can do about it, since this is the life to which they will always be accustomed. When the studio heads give a party, the child has to be dressed up and taken down to mingle with the guests and she is kept up very late.

I'm not sure I could have worked for film stars. Mind you, working for VIPs didn't sound much easier, if Nurse Nancy Vincent's account of her time with the Governor of Jamaica was anything to go by.

My life is busy past imagining. I am caring for the Governor and Lady Foot's three children. We have a continual stream of visitors, some interesting, some a little peculiar. We have entertained the Churchill family, Admirals, Air Marshals, MPs, Charles Laughton, Yehudi Menuhin, Presidents and Ambassadors and now we have HM the Queen and HRH the Duke of Edinburgh with us for nearly three days.

Tremendous preparations are being made. It will mean huge parties, a reception for 2000 people and a dinner party for 100 on the second day. We shall do it all ourselves with a little extra help brought in.

The tradespeople of the island are extraordinarily kind. They hold our Governor in great esteem and I have only to ask and they offer me all I could wish for within their limits.

Mind you, I'm pleased to say my contemporaries weren't just helping the privileged. Many, still so touched by their experiences during the war, gave up their private posts in the 1950s and 60s to care for orphans in Barnardo's homes, work in Church of England homes for destitute children, look after dockers' children in the bomb-scarred East End or help care for children permanently injured through war.

One brave Norlander even visited and worked in shelters, camps, orphanages, a school for the deaf and speech-impaired, a mother-and-baby home, a girls' remand home, a boys' hostel, homes for refugees or vagabonds or for the chronically sick, *and* public health centres . . . phew . . . in war-torn Germany!

'One cannot possibly compare conditions in our own institutions with those that now exist in Germany,' Nurse Jean Woolridge wrote.

The biggest problem, aside from money, is that of refugees. There are so many people from the Eastern Zone just 'wandering' throughout the country, parted from their families and their homes. No links, no roots, and yet they are the rising generation.

177

I shall never forget the 'Bunker House' we visited. The walls were 6ft deep, with not a single window. One electric ring for three families and no hot water. It was dark, overcrowded and stifling. 400 people were crammed into these conditions, and yet the majority of the small cubicles, which are shared by the whole family, are spotless. These proud housewives' standard of cleanliness is very high.

I also was touched by visiting an orphanage housed in a former Luftwaffe Barracks. 350 orphans from 1 to 16 are housed in a most unsuitable building. There are only 50 staff to care for them all and hot water only twice a week. Such overcrowded and dreadful conditions I never knew existed. Unemployment is high, and there is so much rebuilding to be done, although it is impossible to build new houses because of the high cost. They try to repair the houses but one only has to visit Germany to see there is so much still untouched.

Accounts such as these from my fellow nurses really made one stop and think of the devastation that the war had caused, not just to us here in England, but to the poor mothers and children still struggling in Germany. They hadn't asked for that dreadful war any more than we had.

The nurses' accounts in the newsletter really were tales of extremes, from children who lived in unimaginable desperation and poverty to those with lives of unadulterated privilege and comfort. Such is the nature of life, I suppose.

Did I hanker for a life abroad, working for film stars or

helping to arrange parties for the Queen? Honestly, no. Besides, the home county and Chelsea sets kept me very busy. Lovely ladies like Judith Beecroft, Marjorie Wadell and Anne Wigglesworth all entrusted me with their first, then second and then third babies.

Mothers have told me how they worry that they can't possibly love a second child as much as their first. And then of course they give birth and they do love them every bit as much. In many ways being a troubleshooting nanny is just the same. With every child I cared for, my capacity for love expanded, my heart growing bigger with every fresh new life cradled in my arms.

'Come back soon, you're a valued member of our family, you can't be surpassed, no one will take your place,' the mothers cried, but no amount of compliments could persuade me to stay. There were simply too many babies to love.

I never grew bored, restless or tired of my profession, and that is the wonderful thing about being a nanny. Every day is so different, every child unique – how could I ever tire of such a challenge?

While others were learning how to do the twist in Mary Quant miniskirts and a revolution in fashion and music swept over London, I remained blissfully ignorant. A lot of the time these changes were going on right under my nose, in the heart of swinging Chelsea, but my nurseries were quiet, innocent, timeless places and not for a moment did I yearn to be outside their hallowed walls. It would take more than a flash young man in a Mini to lure me away from my babies.

Of course, the helpless little babies I winded, fed and paced nurseries with night after night in the 1960s are now all grown-up, with important jobs of their own.

One little boy I cared for on a number of occasions, who could never pronounce his little sister Sarah's name and always called her 'Pooargh', overcame his stumbling start and is now an eminent barrister who speaks most eloquently and commandingly in a courtroom.

Another child, a little girl called Fiona, who used to totter around the nursery after me in the late 1970s calling 'Nannee, Nannee,' I recognised when I opened the paper the other day and saw her smiling back at me, a radiant bride flanked by her usher, Prince William, his new wife Catherine and his sister-in-law Pippa.

Fiona might be a society girl now, but to me she'll always be a dear little girl who loved cuddles.

But money, we all know, can't buy you happiness, as I found when I encountered dear Charlotte Munroe in 1961.

Charlotte lived in Chelsea with her husband and they had been married for ten years. Now in her late thirties, she had been trying since the day after they got married to conceive. Ten years of heartache, questioning, endless tests and soul-searching.

The IVF procedures that answer the prayers of so many couples today were a long way off then. Back in the 1960s couples couldn't rely on medical science to intervene and it had looked very likely that Charlotte was set to become another statistic filed under 'unexplained infertility'.

'It was agonising,' she confessed to me now, cradling her little girl Poppy as though she was made of precious porcelain. 'All those years and nothing. Sheer and utter misery, Nurse Brenda. You begin to question everything. We did everything the doctors suggested: we ate healthily, didn't drink, took regular exercise. Doctors could find no medical reason why I couldn't conceive and yet, month after month, year after torturous year, my period came, as regular as clockwork, and with it our hopes were cruelly dashed.'

'You poor, poor thing,' I murmured.

And yet here I was, gazing at her holding her sweet baby tenderly in her arms, looking for all the world as if she might melt with love. I dare say no baby was ever wanted more. Charlotte was utterly captivated, spellbound by the precious bundle before her.

'So what happened?' I asked. 'If you don't mind my asking.'

She shrugged. 'It's a mystery, Nurse Brenda. One day, after all these years, the test simply came back positive. I did nothing different and yet finally our prayers were answered.'

The atmosphere in the pastel-pink nursery was one of utter serenity, and I smiled as I saw how Charlotte couldn't resist constantly planting soft kisses on her baby's head, almost as if to reassure herself that her baby was real and not just a figment of her imagination.

'I'll say this though,' she added, glancing up at me as she stroked Charlotte's velvet-soft cheek with her finger. 'I never gave up hope or lost faith. Not once. I knew I'd be a mother someday. We've had this room decorated as a nursery for ten years. Day after day I'd come in here and imagine myself sitting in here, nursing my baby.'

Perhaps that was the secret of her success? Perhaps by wanting something so much, and by visualising herself as a mother, she had made it happen. Summoned up a miracle? Who knew, but it was a potent reminder never to give up on your hopes and dreams.

Charlotte had money, that much was obvious from the smart house in a very desirable postcode, but she had a far more powerful weapon in her possession. Faith.

I was with Charlotte and Poppy for one month and rarely has a job filled me with such satisfaction and happiness. Charlotte had a thirst for knowledge and squeezed my brain like a sponge.

'I want to know everything there is to know about babies, Nurse Brenda, no detail is too small,' she said.

Charlotte was so hands-on, wanting everything done correctly and in the proper manner. There was no grumbling about how tired she was or bemoaning her lack of freedom, just endless bottle-washing, nappy-changing, winding, feeding and all the other labour-intensive jobs that make up the rigorous routine dominating a newborn baby's life.

'This is all I've ever wanted, Nurse Brenda,' she told me when I tried to hustle her back to bed with a cup of tea for some rest. 'I don't want to be parted from her for a second. It sounds crazy, but I miss her when she's in the next room.'

So instead of taking over, I was the support act, gently showing her how to bathe, burp and care for her little miracle. Going on that journey of discovery with her as she felt her way round motherhood and got to know her baby's likes and dislikes was an honour.

On the last night she was triumphant. 'I've worked out, Nurse Brenda, that if I hold her across my knees with her tummy down it seems to soothe her trapped wind.'

As she softly patted Poppy's back, I grinned. 'Well done you,' I cheered. 'You're a total professional now. You don't need me any longer.'

By the time I left her, when Poppy the miracle turned four weeks old, they were both flourishing.

Mr and Mrs Steiner lived in London and had just had occasion to celebrate the birth of their first child, a son they planned on calling Benjamin. The occasion was obviously momentous, and the little boy was every bit as treasured as Charlotte's baby.

'I might be biased,' gushed the lady of the house, once she had welcomed me in. 'But he really is the most perfect little baby I've ever seen. He's so good.'

I smiled. To every parent their little baby is quite simply the most perfect, adorable and exquisite creation in history.

This one was a treasure, though. Benjamin was just two days old and his eyes were clamped tightly shut. He looked as though he was concentrating very hard indeed on sleeping and planned to do so for the foreseeable future. Bless him. He didn't even know he was out of the womb.

It's funny how some people imagine that all new babies do is scream lustily at the tops of their lungs until they're blue in the face. In reality they spend most of their days sleeping, oblivious to the fact that they're even born.

Cradling her son gently in her arms, Mrs Steiner shook her head in wonder. 'I can hardly believe he's mine,' she whispered, instinctively rocking backwards and forwards to soothe the sleeping babe. 'My husband's over the moon to have a son.'

Anyone would be over the moon to have this sleeping angel as their child. Benjamin had a complexion like double cream. Little tendrils of soft dark hair curled gently round his tiny ears and five tiny little fingers were curled tightly round one of his mother's. We talked over my duties and every now and again Benjamin sighed or snuffled gently and Mrs Steiner would freeze, like she'd just dropped a Picasso, until he snuggled back down into her arms.

Smiling softly, I marvelled at the strength of this magical love between mother and child and retreated quietly from the room, careful not to interrupt their delicate bonding process.

'I'll be unpacking in my room,' I murmured.

Mrs Steiner didn't even look up, so busy was she gazing at her most precious possession.

Later, once I'd packed my things away and Benjamin was sleeping in his cot, Mrs Steiner and I talked over my appointment in more detail.

'My husband and I are Orthodox Jews, Nurse Brenda, and while you are here we will have our son circumcised as well as partake in a number of special ceremonies and dinners.'

I gulped. I didn't approve of this practice. It seemed unnecessary and cruel in my opinion, but I wasn't being paid for my opinions so I kept my mouth shut and merely nodded politely.

'Every Friday night my husband and I have dinner with my father-in-law and the rest of our family and we would love it if you could join us,' she went on. 'We'd love you to feel like a member of this family while you're with us.'

I nodded and smiled. 'I'd be delighted.'

On the first Friday we duly got ready, gently placing their little baby boy in his smart coach pram and tucking him in under snowy white blankets before we all walked the short distance to Mr Steiner's parents' house in Wimpole Street, in the heart of the City of Westminster.

Today this area, which is also home to Harley Street, is teeming with private medical practices, but back in the 1960s the soaring five-storey townhouses were private homes to millionaires. Unbeknownst to me, a young Paul McCartney and John Lennon were penning many of their hit songs in the attic of the family home of Paul's then girlfriend Jane Asher at number 57 Wimpole Street.

While 'I Want To Hold Your Hand' drifted down from a loft room, we walked right on past and arrived at the door of number 6 Wimpole Street.

I'd already gleaned a little information about Mr and Mrs Steiner Senior. Mr Steiner had arrived in England from Austria as a penniless Jew at the outbreak of the Second World War. He'd been running from Hitler's barbaric regime and had arrived in London with not a penny to his name, literally just the shirt on his back.

As I admired the imposing redbrick townhouse with its enormous black door flanked by stone lions, I marvelled at the sheer determination that must have gone into working his way up from penniless refugee to millionaire owner of this impressive property in just twenty years.

'My father worked hard on a stall when he first arrived in London,' explained Mr Steiner, noticing my obvious admiration of his father's home. 'Before long what little money he had saved he invested in a shoe factory in the north of England. He worked harder still, reinvested, and well, the rest is history. Now he owns a whole string of luxury shoe shops across England.'

As I stared up at the house I felt quite dizzy and gripped the pram handles for support. It really was amazing and I felt quite in awe of this impressive gentleman and his even more impressive home.

He could have allowed his circumstances to defeat him. Brutalised for his religion, he could have arrived here and felt overwhelmed and bitter after being forced to flee his homeland. Instead he poured every ounce of his fibre into building up his business and inventing a new future for himself.

Thinking about refugees, I found my mind wandering back to a lovely little evacuee called Gretal whom I had cared for during the war. Gretal, like Mr Steiner, was an Austrian Jew forced to flee her homeland. She had been just one of 10,000 Jewish children wrenched from their families at the outbreak of the war to avoid Nazi persecution.

The poor little treasure, no older than five, had been painfully shy, and no matter how many times I'd tried to reach out to her she'd shrunk back from my touch, bewildered, lost and quite alone in her misery.

'Mama, mama,' she'd cried over and over. 'I want Mama.' Not for the first time during the war my heart had broken at the mistreatment of children. In my eyes they were the forgotten victims of the war, and little Gretal was the reason we were all fighting and sacrificing so much to save our country from tyranny. I tried so hard to raise a smile in her serious little face, but as she didn't speak much English beyond the word 'Mama' it was impossible.

Finally, I had used humour to win her over and gain her trust. Thanks to some marvellous duck and lion impressions from me and the other evacuees we'd coaxed a wonderful throaty little giggle from her. When I'd eventually left her to go to a new job two years later she was still shy, but I like to think she no longer felt alone.

Now I found myself wondering where Gretal was. She'd be twenty-three by now, a grown woman. Had she returned to Austria or stayed, learned the language and put down roots like Mr Steiner? Did she remember the nanny who had played games with her, given her her weekly bath in a tin tub and done silly animal impressions to cheer her up?

In fact did any of the evacuees I'd so lovingly read *Rupert the Bear* to in front of a roaring fire as the war raged on around us remember me? It was a mystery and it was destined to stay that way for ever.

So many intense relationships formed in the war years were lost on the winds of time. Gretal would be forever frozen in my memory as a shy five-year-old forced apart from her Mama. How I prayed she'd found success and good fortune in our country like Mr Steiner obviously had.

The door swung open and Mr Steiner Senior, millionaire factory-owner, a small man almost as wide as he was tall, beamed back at us. His little blue eyes twinkled with merriment and joviality.

'Good Shabbos,' he said in a rich, welcoming voice. 'And welcome to my home, Nurse Brenda.'

Instinctively I liked this man. He may have ruled over an empire and a fleet of staff, but when it came to his grandson he was reduced to a pile of mush.

'How is my beautiful boy?' he boomed, swooping in and plucking his grandson from the coach pram. 'We are very lucky, are we not, nurse Brenda, to have such a miracle in our midst.' And with that he kissed his grandson tenderly on the head and gazed into his eyes, utterly captivated.

The rest of the evening was a joy. The household was beyond plush but it was the family who made it so impressive. There was family everywhere – cousins, aunts, uncles – all babbling away ten to the dozen in a riot of noise, laughter and chatter. I could scarcely believe they all belonged to the same family. Once we were seated round the table in a huge wood-panelled dining room I counted forty people in all.

All the men were dressed smartly in their best suits, and the women had taken great care with their clothes. The house had been polished until it sparkled, and the best dinner service had been laid out. Dozens of candles lit the room, casting a soft glow across their faces.

The noise created by this larger-than-life family was deafening. I marvelled at how baby Benjamin, in his pram in the corner of the room, could sleep through it all. Mind you, having witnessed children sound asleep underground while deafening German bombs exploded overhead, I wasn't that surprised. Babies and children may like to wake adults in the night, but when they are in the land of nod, nothing wakes them.

'Friday evenings are very important to us,' explained Mrs Steiner, who was seated to my right. 'As Austrian Jews we are what's known as Ashkenazi Jews, and Friday is a Jewish holiday called Shabbos. We observe this most keenly from sunset on Fridays.

'Many people think of it as a day of restrictions, as we do not work during Shabbos, or turn on a television, drive a car or go shopping for example, but this is misguided. Instead it is a time of rest and spiritual enrichment. It's a time of great joy eagerly awaited throughout the week, a time when we can set aside all our weekday concerns, come together with our family and devote ourselves to higher pursuits.'

I nodded earnestly. I was impressed that she was taking the time to explain her faith to me and include me, so I had a duty to try to listen and understand. I may have been of a different faith and worshipped when I could at a Baptist church, but I still enjoyed hearing about religions. It is always impressive when someone is thoughtful enough to try and include you.

'Why do the men always wear black?' I asked.

'Good question, Nurse Brenda.' She smiled. 'There is no requirement to wear black. Many Jews – Orthodox or otherwise – dress in a traditionally Jewish manner simply to make it obvious that they are Jews. Judaism has been around for several thousand years and the Jewish people have contributed a very great deal to human knowledge and ethics, so many Jews feel pride in being Jewish. It maintains our distinct identity, it gives a uniform appearance and evens everyone out.'

I nodded, fascinated. As someone who had trained and spent a great deal of time in uniform I certainly could relate to the desire to wear a uniform and feel part of something bigger.

'Jewish men wear the black hats as a sign of mourning because the holy temple that was destroyed in Jerusalem has not been rebuilt,' she went on. 'We believe in the Torah. It is amazing when you consider that the Jewish people were in exile for more than two thousand years in every corner of the earth, creating different traditions and costumes, but when the Jewish state was created they all came with the exact same Bible, not a single letter was changed.'

Once we were all seated a variety of songs were sung, first by everyone, then just by the men.

'Why are just the men singing?' I whispered to Mrs Steiner.

'They are singing a song written by King Solomon to honour their wives and show their gratitude,' she explained.

After that her mother-in-law and a host of other women brought in plates of bread and steaming tureens of delicious-smelling soup.

'My father-in-law will bless this special bread, known as challah, and then once we have eaten that, chicken soup will be served,' explained Mrs Steiner.

Everyone looked at Mr Steiner, seated at the head of the table, and waited expectantly.

Irritation flashed over his usually jovial face. 'Where's my kippa?' he asked.

'The fabric hat he wears,' said Mrs Steiner helpfully. 'Jewish men wear it as a sign of respect for God and recognition that there is someone above us who watches our every act.'

'Where's my kippa?' he muttered, growing gradually more red of face. Chairs were scraped back and there was much scratching of heads and hunting as everyone tried to locate it.

Meanwhile Mr Steiner grew crosser, his round face going red with rage as he huffed and puffed. Eventually he shook his head, exasperated, and grabbed the nearest thing he could find, which happened to be a neatly folded copy of the *Telegraph* on a side table. Placing the newspaper over his head, and lifting the loaves of bread in his other hand, he began to bless the meal in Hebrew.

His mouth reverently mouthed the special blessing as all the while he clutched the newspaper over his head. My eyes widened and it was all I could do not to burst into fits of giggles at this extraordinary sight. Sensing my amazement Mrs Steiner smiled.

'For an Orthodox Jew he can be a little unorthodox at times,' she whispered.

The incident was quite forgotten a few minutes later. With the meal blessed, everyone tucked into the feast. Bread was broken and shared, then, after that was eaten, piping hot soup was ladled into dishes and wine poured. All the while the group wished each other 'Good Shabbos.'

Everyone talked, laughed, ate leisurely and told stories. The room hummed with warmth, respect and companionship. I doubted a single member of this family ever felt alone or starved of love. And then it hit me. A sense of camaraderie may have been breaking down on the streets outside, but it was alive and kicking here in this house.

The Steiners weren't just a family, they were a self-contained community! That night I went to sleep snug, warm and more alive than I'd felt in years. For the first time since Mother's death and since I'd begun my troubleshooting mission six years earlier, I was witnessing family life at its richest, noisiest, most chaotic and irrepressible. It was a joy to behold.

But a few days later, when little Benjamin was exactly eight days old, I was informed he was to be circumcised.

'We call it the Brit Milah,' explained Mrs Steiner. 'For three and a half thousand years, since the time of our forefather Abraham, the Jewish people have observed the ritual of circumcision as the fundamental sign of the covenant between God and Israel. To us it's much more than a simple medical procedure. Brit Milah is considered the sign of a new-born male child's entry into the Jewish tradition. For millennia, in every country where Jews have lived they have always practised this ritual. Brit Milah is the ultimate affirmation of Jewish identity.'

Benjamin's snoozy, sleepy existence and the peace of the nursery were shattered when the mohel arrived – a man medically trained to perform the Brit Milah, but also a man possessed of great piety and religiosity.

'It's time,' said Mrs Steiner when she entered the nursery, accompanied by a man and a woman. I felt sick to my stomach as I lifted little Benjamin from his warm and cosy nest and handed him, still sleeping, to his mother. From there Benjamin was ceremoniously handed to the woman. 'This is Benjamin's godmother, or as we call her, the kvatterin, and this is his godfather, the kvatter,' she explained.

From there they carried him to a different room where Mr Steiner, the mohel and another spiritually important man, known as the sandek, were waiting to begin the ceremony.

I wanted to leap up after them, pluck little Benjamin back from their arms and bring him back to the nursery. Instead I sat motionless in a chair.

Minutes later an almighty howl rang out around the house. Oh my, the cries of pain! It made me feel sick to my core. The poor little poppet's cry nearly lifted the rafters.

Sickness was replaced by anger. It seemed barbaric, hurting a baby for no good reason.

I could hear the mohel reciting a special blessing over a cup of wine and Benjamin was officially given his Hebrew name.

As the rest of the party went to the dining room for a kosher meal, as is customary, Mrs Steiner brought Benjamin back to the nursery. She took one look at my stricken face and frowned.

'It's perfectly normal, Nurse Brenda, please don't worry,' she soothed. 'He'll be back to normal before long.'

Before I could help myself the words were out of my mouth. 'Well I'm afraid I don't go along with this one little bit,' I muttered. It wasn't like me to say something like that, but something inside me felt compelled.

She said nothing, just handed Benjamin to me. His tiny body was rigid with pain and he was shaking . . . actually shaking.

'Oh my darling,' I soothed, rubbing his back as he trembled in my arms. I stayed that way, gently calming and patting him until his cries grew less ferocious.

By the time he fell into an exhausted sleep I was spent. I knew as a nanny it wasn't my position to judge, but, well, I simply couldn't help it. It was against my every instinct to stand witness to a child's suffering, however small. But true enough, he did recover quickly and my outburst wasn't mentioned again.

On the thirty-first day of Benjamin's life he took part in another ceremony. As always, Mrs Steiner explained what was happening to me.

'The ritual of redemption is referred to as Pidyon Ha-ben, which literally means "redemption of the son". My husband will pay a priest five silver shekels so that Benjamin is released from the obligation to serve in the temple.'

My face must have been a picture of confusion.

'Don't worry, Nurse Brenda,' she laughed. 'He wouldn't actually have worked in a temple. It's a symbolic gesture. In Exodus 13:2 it is written "Sanctify unto Me every first-born, whatsoever openeth the womb among the children of Israel, both of man and of beast: it is Mine". In remembrance of how God spared the firstborn sons of Israel, He declared that all firstborn sons belonged to Him. By symbolically paying a priest, we are releasing Benjamin from his obligation to serve in a temple. Most firstborn Jewish sons will go through this ceremony.'

I watched, mesmerised, from the corner of the living room as Benjamin, still fast asleep in his smart white silk Babygro, was slowly and solemnly brought into the room by his father on a silver tray decorated with jewellery, sugar cubes and garlic. Lying in the middle of all this on a satin cushion, curled up asleep, Benjamin looked so beautiful. A serene yet serious atmosphere filled the room. I hardly dared breathe.

'That man is a holy man known as the kohen. He's a member of a priestly family,' whispered Mrs Steiner. 'The sugar cubes represent that the commandments are sweet and the garlic is a symbol of fertility.'

'Is this child your firstborn son?' the kohen solemnly asked Mr Steiner.

'He is,' confirmed Mr Steiner.

'Which do you prefer, to give me your firstborn or to redeem him?' asked the kohen.

My eyes widened. Surely no parent would give their child to a priest?

'I wish to redeem him,' answered Mr Steiner, and with that he handed the kohen five silver coins. I breathed out slowly in relief as Mr Steiner began to chant in a slow and steady voice.

After that the atmosphere lightened and everyone smiled.

'Let's eat,' declared Mr Steiner, tenderly taking his son off the silver tray and handing him to me.

I couldn't pretend for a minute to really understand all that was going on, but it was fascinating, and I felt privileged to be included in these ancient traditions and customs.

It was like no other house I'd ever worked in, but I loved that in every home I passed through I learned a little more of what makes the world go round. What stirs, motivates and guides people on life's journey. I didn't agree with circumcision, true, but I could see how close and bonded the Steiners were, and how little Benjamin was adored and worshipped by his extended family. What better upbringing for a child?

It wasn't until a few days later that I really saw how the Jewish faith came into its own. I was doing the washing-up one morning when I happened to see, through the kitchen window, a steady stream of Jewish men and women troop-ing up to a neighbour's house, each of them carrying a dish.

'What are they doing?' I asked Mrs Steiner.

She peered over my shoulder. 'Ah,' she said. 'Those are our neighbours, and sadly they are sitting shiva. There has been a death in the family next door and the seven-day period of mourning after the death is known as sitting shiva. Everyone in the community will come and visit them to pay their respects.'

'What are they carrying?' I asked.

'Bowls of food,' she replied. 'Lentil- or egg-based food mainly. The eggs refer to the circle of life. It is a great comfort for the family to know they are not alone.'

I watched in wonder as all day people came to pay their respects, and then left. Not a single person came without food. A continual stream of food and love poured into that house.

Shortly after that my appointment came to an end and my time with the Steiner family was over, but I shall never forget it. Not least for the respect they showed me by including me in their faith and taking the trouble to explain it, but also for helping me to realise that communities *do* still exist. It was most heartening to see their community rally round the grieving, welcome a new life into the world and take the time to sit and eat meals together.

I've always said that if you live in a community you must contribute to that community. The Jewish faith is a shining example of how to do it well.

Soon after I took my leave of this family I had another call. A quite desperate call, in fact.

'I need you, Nurse Brenda. Please say you'll come, you will come, won't you? I don't know what I'll do if you can't, honestly, I'm quite beside myself,' the voice babbled.

'Slow down, slow down,' I soothed. 'Who is this?'

'It's Charlotte Munroe, Nurse Brenda.'

'Charlotte,' I exclaimed. 'What a lovely surprise. How are you and Poppy?'

'We're fine,' she replied. There was a long pause, then: 'I'm pregnant.'

'Well, well, well,' I chuckled. 'Who'd have thought it?'

After everything she'd been through, all those desperate years of waiting, hoping and trying, now this.

'There's something else,' she added. 'It's twins.'

The medical world can explain a lot and seems to know the answer to most things these days, but I still say there is no greater mystery in life than a woman's body. Quite why now, after all this time, Charlotte's body was able to conceive not just one baby but three in such a short space of time was anyone's guess.

'Unexplained fertility,' the doctors called it. A miracle I called it.

And so, in 1962 I once again found myself in Chelsea. As I knocked on the door I could very clearly hear the unmistakeable sound of hungry babies crying out to be fed. Three sets of lungs were roaring at top volume.

The twins were four weeks old and by my reckoning Poppy was only eleven months. Charlotte was in the unenviable position of being a mother to three babies all under the age of one.

Charlotte looked exhausted and yet radiant when she flung open the door. A faint stain of baby vomit was smeared on the shoulder of her blouse and her eyes were ringed with dark circles. But there was no mistaking the look of utter love and peace that shone from her eyes.

'Sheer joy and relief to have you here, Nurse Brenda,' she gushed, gripping my hand and pulling me in. 'I can't even begin to tell you. I was terrified I might not get you, but here you are. Nurse Ashford to the rescue.'

In the nursery I could see I was going to have my work cut out.

Poppy, Peter and Alice were lying on a little rug on the nursery floor, all competing for who could make the most noise.

'Gracious,' I chuckled. 'What a lot of hungry babies we have here.'

'Help me,' pleaded Charlotte. 'Who do I go to first? I've been getting in the most dreadful muddle.'

'Routine is the key here,' I said calmly, taking out my trusty pad and paper and jotting down a note of the feeding time. 'For now, I will help position Peter on one of your breasts and Alice on the other to feed, but in future we'll have to start staggering their feed times or you will quickly become exhausted. And as we all know, an exhausted mother is not a happy one.'

When the twins were feeding happily I prepared a bottle for Poppy and peace was finally restored to the nursery.

Charlotte's eyelids began to close as her shoulders relaxed and she lay back against her chair, her twins suckling happily at her breast.

'So relieved to have you . . .' she sighed. But she didn't finish her sentence, because a second later she was sound asleep.

I smiled as I waited for all the babies to finish their feeds.

You are going to have your work cut out for you here, Brenda, I said to myself.

I won't pretend it was easy, but over the coming month I soon had that nursery whipped into shape. We made up a feeding chart to be placed on the wall, as we used to do when I worked at Great Ormond Street Hospital, and I was meticulous about settling the twins into a routine and sticking to feed times.

All the babies were lined up on the floor to have their nappies changed. How it made us giggle to see six chubby legs sticking up into the air, and the sound of their delighted squeals and gurgles as I played peekaboo was triple the fun.

Our days were never terribly ambitious. One short walk out after lunch so Charlotte could take a nap was about all I could manage, all three snuggled shoulder to shoulder into a spacious coach pram.

Night-times were a little harder. I still insisted on being the one to get up in the night.

'That is *my* job and I really must put my foot down,' I said when Charlotte tried to protest. 'You'll need all your strength for the coming years.'

Poppy was sleeping through by then, but the twins certainly took it in turns to keep me active during the night-time hours. No sooner were my eyes closing and I was drifting off than a baby's cry would wrench me from my sleep.

But as I sat in the darkened nursery, looking out on to the deserted streets below, I realised with a jolt that I had been troubleshooting for six years and a nanny for twenty-two. On the whole, eight hours' uninterrupted sleep was a distant memory.

The wind whispered through the branches of the tree outside the nursery, casting long spooky shadows on to the road below. A fox slunk out of the dark, on the prowl. Three a.m. is the witching hour and I'd seen it more times than I cared to remember. Not a soul stirred. Except for a nanny quietly going about her business.

As baby Alice greedily sucked at the bottle I was giving her I allowed my thoughts to wander.

I'd seen babies presented to priests on silver dishes, helped to dispose of dead pigs, had run screaming from a mad heifer, dealt with jealous mothers, avoided the advances of lecherous fathers, soothed a million tantrums, changed twice as many dirty nappies, gasped at con men crawling through the bushes, witnessed the miracle of birth and the unexplained joy of three surprise babies . . . Oh, and taken tea with the Queen Mother.

What's more I had thoroughly enjoyed every chaotic, smelly, wonderful, noisy, life-affirming and explosive moment. But was I ready to settle down? Perhaps stay and help Charlotte out for longer? She had certainly hinted on many an occasion that she would like me to.

Looking out into the dark of the night, I knew with a certainty: *no.* Destiny had plans for me beyond the streets of Chelsea. I wasn't sure when, how or indeed why it would strike, but I felt sure that out there, in the seething metropolis, magic was brewing . . .

Testimonial

Nurse Ashford came to us initially last year to care for our first daughter, during the month following birth. Besides her capable handling of the baby and sincere affection she showed towards her charge, Nurse Ashford imparted to me such knowledge and confidence that, upon her departure, I was able to carry on alone without the qualms I had originally feared. Her methodical ways and cheerful countenance together created the perfect nursery atmosphere and it was with sheer joy and relief that we were able to have Nurse Ashford with us again to take our twin boy and girl during their second month. Three babies under one year is a handful by any standards, but Nurse Ashford understood each one in her own inimitable fashion, and they all flourished under her care and benefited from her experience. We will always wish her well.

Charlotte Munroe

NANNY'S WISDOM

The perfect antidote

All children adore smiles. Sometimes we adults use words children don't understand or talk too fast. Remember, most communication is non-verbal, and at no time is this truer than with little children. Make a point of smiling at children more. It costs nothing but it counts for a lot.

Chivalry costs nothing

I have often talked of the virtue of good manners, but I also believe chivalrous men to be a dying breed. Chivalry dates back to medieval times, when the knightly code embraced such virtues such as courtly love, honour and courteous behaviour.

My father was the ultimate gentleman. He always opened doors for ladies, stood if a lady came into the room, gave up his seat and walked on the side nearest the traffic on the pavement. These are the old-fashioned ideas that I was brought up on and it helped make my parents' marriage stronger, I'm sure.

When was the last time a man gave up his seat or opened a door for you? Do your bit to bring it back by insisting that your sons show deference to girls. If you do it when they're young, it will be natural to them later in life. Respect for the opposite sex is the foundation of good manners.

Impeccable manners are something I always insisted on from my charges and I firmly believe being raised by a chivalrous man helped to instil them in me.

Get your daily constitutional

I'm not saying you should make your children take their naps outside like I used to at the Norland, but I simply cannot overstate the importance of fresh air to children, and adults for that matter. Switch off the mobiles, televisions or computer games and get them outside in the fresh air for a short walk at least once a day. I struggled to keep order in the day at Charlotte Munroe's with so many babies, but I always made sure to get the children out at least once a day.

7

Coming Home

Lavender's blue, dilly dilly, lavender's green,
When I am king, dilly dilly, you shall be queen.
Seventeenth-century nursery rhyme

'Good to have you back,' boomed Mr Gordon, opening the door to his spacious Surrey home. 'Come on in and meet the new arrival.'

It was 1965 and many years had passed since I had first worked for Mr Gordon and his wife. Nine years, to be precise, since that fateful job in Kensington when Mother had passed away. Had she still been alive she wouldn't have recognised London from the place where we had taken tea in the Lyons Corner House all those years ago.

The Beatles were dominating the charts, women's hemlines had risen to almost indecent levels and there was a revolution in fashion, music and sexual behaviour. Girls in Mary Quant miniskirts and go-go boots strode down the King's Road in Chelsea. People shopped in supermarkets, ate sliced bread and lollies on sticks, watched soap operas and bought mass-market, low-quality disposable products. Would Mother have approved? I'm not sure.

I had returned to the Gordons on a number of brief occasions since the twins' births, but had never stayed for more than a few weeks each time. My quest to work for as many families as I possibly could had spurred me on and even now, the day after I had turned forty-four, I had not the slightest inclination to stop. I must have cared for approaching one hundred children, but still the itch wasn't yet scratched.

I had long since given up on finding a man – that boat had sailed for me – and with acceptance came a kind of freedom I could never have imagined. Whilst my contemporaries were taking the pill, forging new careers and travelling more than ever before, I was firmly entrenched in the nursery. But I was at peace with my decisions, a stronger, more confident woman than ever before.

A decade of troubleshooting, of living in other women's homes and caring for their offspring, does that to you.

'Can't we tempt you to stay longer, Nurse Ashford?' said Mrs Gordon. 'The twins are nine and now we have a new baby we really could do with your help.'

I'd heard this kind of plea before from many a mother but I was adamant.

'I'm afraid not,' I smiled. 'I'll stay for six weeks, until you're up on your feet.'

She sighed.

'Oh well. Perhaps you better meet your new charge.'

Suddenly the twins, Belinda and Fiona, rushed in.

'Oh Nana,' they laughed, wrapping their arms round me and smothering me in kisses. 'You've come back.'

'Gracious,' I chuckled, untangling myself from their sticky embraces. 'It's so nice to feel wanted.'

'Do you want to meet our new baby sister, Susanna?' Belinda blurted out, eyes shining. 'Do you? She's very little, just like a real doll.'

'Oh yes please,' I laughed. 'I should like that very much indeed.'

Just then the door to the drawing room swung open and in walked Mr Gordon carrying the nearest thing I had ever seen to a real-life little doll.

'Oh my,' I breathed. 'May I?'

'Of course,' he laughed, gently placing her in my arms.

Only David's birth thirty-five years previously and Pippa's eighteen years ago had ever had such a profound effect on me. Everyone else in the room just seemed to melt away as I locked eyes with this precious pink bundle.

'She's so tiny,' I marvelled. 'Just a little scrap.'

'She was a month premature,' said Mrs Gordon. 'Just five pounds.'

She may have been the size of a tiny porcelain doll, but she was perfect in every single way. I was so filled with wonder I could scarcely take my eyes off her.

Each exquisitely slender little finger was complete with a minuscule fingernail, and her tiny little cheeks were as soft as velvet. Little dark lashes curled out from tiny eyelids as she slept soundly in my arms. Only her lips, like petite rosebuds, twitched in her sleep. Suddenly something startled her and her eyes shot open in surprise and her arms and legs jerked backwards.

I sensed the twins take a step back.

'It's all right,' I whispered. 'She's quite OK. It's called the Moro reflex. She was just startled.'

Baby Susanna gazed up at me with serious eyes. Then

she snuffled, her deep dark eyes gently closed and she snuggled down into my embrace. I felt quite, quite over-whelmed with love.

How could anything so tiny be so perfect?

Holding her tenderly, I was suddenly reminded of every child who had made an impact on my life.

It had started with the wonder of seeing my baby brother David, but so many, many children had influenced me and made me the person I had become: the helpless yet tremen-dously brave children at Great Ormond Street who fought a daily battle with pain; the irrepressible Bethnal Greenies at Hothfield, separated from their parents but making the best of each and every day.

Then there were Benjy and Peter, my darling first charges who never stopped smiling even when the bombs rained down, bewildered Gretal, forced to flee her country by the Nazis, Jimmy the sweetheart brought up in dismal poverty, the Sacks twins, who helped me on my journey, and Pippa, whose first moments on earth I so gratefully shared. Not to mention countless others who had entered and then left my life again, leaving their own indelible marks on my heart.

Each child was unique, but they all shared a robust and brave resilience; they all sparkled with fun and had an endless capacity for love. That is what is so precious about childhood. Love and cherish a little person and you will receive love back ten-fold. What other relationship on earth promises so much magic? Was it any wonder I chose to spend my life surrounded by children, not with a man?

I learned so much from all these little folk: how to be organised, fair, loyal, patient, consistent, reliable, energetic, fun-loving and resourceful, not to mention tenacious.

As I sat cradling this new tiny soul, I was overcome with a rush of devotion for my profession. As a nanny my love hadn't been squandered. Twenty-six years earlier, in 1939, I had received a calling to help overturn tyranny in the nursery. How grateful was I that I had answered it.

Maybe it was this, or maybe it was because Susanna was so tiny and so vulnerable, but holding her in my arms had a powerful effect on me. Love flooded my body. I imagined this must be what a new mother felt, holding her baby for the first time.

In the weeks that followed the bond between us intensified. It was most extraordinary. Susanna yelped when strangers tried to hold her and clung to me. Even her own father in his smart dark suit got short shrift, but when nestled in my arms she was as good as gold.

As far as I was concerned she was the best thing since this sliced bread I'd been seeing on the shelves. And when six weeks was up, could I leave? Nothing on earth would have dragged me from her side.

Bonds between humans are a most mysterious thing. Why then, after years of holding babies, did such a powerful bond form between Susanna and me? What chemistry ran between us that made me feel compelled to give up from my fleet-footed ways? Why now, after all these years, did I feel the need to settle down?

The urge to nurture and protect is the most powerful instinct in mankind. Perhaps there was something about her fragile little body that tugged at my heartstrings and made me vow to remain by her side. And remain by her side I did. When the six weeks were up, not one word was said by either side. It remained an unspoken agreement. It was time to settle down.

It's a curious life being a nanny and my time with darling Susanna made me realise that living in another family's home is a little like living in a fishbowl. Living cheek by jowl with them you get to share their triumphs, their joys, their successes, but sadly, also their failures.

More or less as soon as we all had settled into our rhythms and new roles I could see that all was not well in the Gordons' marriage.

Mr Gordon had risen through the ranks and was now a well-known and highly respected consultant gynaecologist and obstetrician. He never said more than was absolutely necessary but I knew he was possessed of an extremely kind heart. Now, though, he was positively gruff and after a long day at the hospital he would come in, give the children a kiss and as soon as dinner was over at 9.30 p.m. he would retire to bed.

I had a bad feeling about all this. Fear clutched my heart. What was happening here? I was supposed to be filling this home with love and happiness, and yet the only atmosphere pervading these rooms was one of icy tension.

I felt for Mrs Gordon, really I did. I sensed she was unhappy. She was a lovely lady who absolutely doted on her girls, but it was as if a light had gone out in those pale blue eyes.

Later, in bed, sleep escaped me as I turned my difficulties over and over in my mind. This situation felt so out of my control. I knew their marriage problems weren't my business. I was there to care for Susanna, full stop. And yet

I couldn't shake the feeling that somehow I was part of the problem, not the solution. This was simply unthinkable for me and went against everything I stood for.

It was an unfathomable situation. I remembered my old motto: 'Happy mother, Happy home.'

I found my mind wandering back to the memorable Mrs Trump, the fearsome East End mother of twelve whose little boy I had looked after at the day nursery. That woman had lived in unimaginable poverty, surrounded by squalor and filth with barely enough food to put in her children's mouths. And yet I quite often heard her loud cackle before I saw her fearsome body stomp round the corner.

Like many of her fellow East End mothers she liked a laugh and seemed to find the ribald fun in most situations. Hitler held no fear for that redoubtable mother and her tribe of children. One could only stand in awe of women like Gladys. Life had dealt them a cruel blow but they didn't whinge or moan, they just got on with it with their own spicy, mischievous brand of humour.

Even when Gladys had been telling me off for bathing her precious son she'd done so with a slight gleam of mischief in her eyes. And that time she sewed him into his clothes to prevent him from coming into contact with water, she'd been positively triumphant. Somehow, despite their miserable starts in life and the bad hand they had been dealt with, Gladys Trump and her twelve children squeezed every last drop of fun and humour out of their lives.

There had to be a way to help Mr and Mrs Gordon. My poor old brain was whirling by the time I drifted off into a fitful sleep.

During the weeks and months that followed things deteriorated.

The more unhappy the household became, the more it sent me towards little Susanna. She was growing up to be a shy but terribly sweet little girl who lived for her ponies, and I did my utmost to shield her from the pain of her parents' failing marriage.

By night I rather spoilt her. She simply couldn't settle if she knew I wasn't outside the door. 'Are you there, Nana, are you there?' her little voice cried out across the landing.

Settled outside her door I whispered back, 'I'm right here, sweetheart. Right here.' As if I could possibly be anywhere else.

By day we'd spend hours walking through the fields collecting pretty leaves, making chocolate cake or reading her favourite books, *Black Beauty*, *Anne of Green Gables* and *Swallows and Amazons*. All children can lose themselves in the adventure, freedom and magic of stories, and something about those books provided us with the perfect way to escape the house and allowed our imaginations to run riot. Whether it was the adventures of a tall and untidy tomboy forever getting into trouble but wishing to be loved in *What Katy Did Next*, or the scrapes that John, Susan and Titty got up to while battling piracy on Wild Cat Island, we were hooked.

But it was *Black Beauty* she loved the most. I knew she loved it because she was horse-mad, but I realised as I read it that adults could learn much from this classic story. Values like loyalty, respect and how to treat others with love and kindness shone through.

There is much that can be learned by adults in children's books. We may scoff at these books now and at authors like Enid Blyton and Arthur Ransome for their naive outlook on the world, but to me their stories are excellent ways of teaching children right from wrong and how to behave as a valued member of society. I half wished I could read *Black Beauty* to her parents – in fact to all parents.

But all the books and cakes in the world couldn't shield Susanna from the realities of what was going on under her own roof.

Throughout it all I kept my opinions to myself. In stressful situations I often found myself thinking, what would Mother do? At times I could almost hear her gentle voice in my ear. 'Don't interfere, Brenda, it's not your place. Leave them to resolve their own matters.'

Barbara Castle was appointed Minister of Transport in 1965. Female workers at Ford's in Dagenham went on strike to demand equal pay. Women now expected and indeed demanded equal rights. I watched all these changes on the Gordons' new colour television with growing amazement. I knew they were a good thing but it was all so far removed from my world and in some ways I still felt stuck in the 1940s. But there were other things troubling me.

Man could walk on the moon, English men could hold aloft the World Cup trophy and women could break through into male-dominated worlds, and yet couples couldn't resolve their differences. To me it was utterly baffling.

Matters of the heart were so complicated. Not for the

first time I found myself marvelling at my parents' own marriage. They had made happiness seem so, well, easy. And yet from what I could see a marriage was like a job or a well-kept garden, it needed to be worked at continually in order for it to flourish and survive. Little wonder you're alone, Brenda, I thought to myself one evening. It seems far safer.

At times I realised life probably had been a little easier during wartime. At least we'd all had a clear and common enemy and we all knew our roles in life. That kind of danger, outside the home, you could run and hide from in underground shelters, but unhappiness within the home? Where does one hide then?

By the time Susanna was nine years old the strain had finally taken its toll and sadly Mr and Mrs Gordon parted. I can't even really remember her going as such. I think it must have been a day like any other. All I know was that waves of misery washed over my body. Mr and Mrs Gordon's divorce felt in some ways like a personal failure. It was, after all, the first divorce I had encountered amongst the parents of my charges.

I had set out all those years ago with the intention of supporting mothers and helping to make their homes the happiest places they could possibly be. I had failed.

Worry and fear began to stalk me. Was Susanna too attached to me? Had I allowed my overwhelming love for that little girl to cloud my professional judgement? Questions raced through my mind at breakneck speed, but no matter how hard I tried to reason it out there were simply no answers.

A terrible dark cloud of fear and anxiety seemed to

hover over me at all times. It was the first thing I thought of in the morning and the last thing I thought of at night. It even stalked my dreams.

When I had been running from Hitler's bombs, or heard a V-1 flying bomb droning overhead, I hadn't felt this terrible feeling of doom deep down in the pit of my tummy. Bringing happiness to the home was *everything* to me, I had staked my professional reputation on it. Without love and happiness what else is there in life?

It was all just too terrible for words. Perhaps it would be better all round if I simply packed my bags and went. Upped sticks and left like I had all those times in the past? It would be easy, but did that make it right?

Not knowing where else to turn, I visited Susanna's headmistress, a sensible lady who would, I knew, offer me good advice.

'What should I do?' I asked. 'My role is to support the mother, not replace her.'

After I had blurted out the rest of the sorry story, she smiled at me. 'Brenda, I feel for you, I really do. But I would urge you to stay.'

Something about this kindly lady with her soft voice and half-moon spectacles seemed to inspire trust. Sitting in headmistress's offices had always unnerved me, ever since, aged sixteen, I had marched into my old headmistress's office to inform her I would no longer be continuing my education. But this lady had Susanna's best interests at heart, just like me.

'Susanna needs some continuity and stability in her life now more than ever,' she went on. 'This is a crucial time.'

Walking home I realised with a sharp stab how much I

missed my mother. She would have known just the right things to say and do. A cup of tea and a slice of knight's pudding in her warm and cosy kitchen was just what I needed right now. I didn't like to burden Kathleen with my problems. I suspected she was suffering with her own depression. But oh, what I wouldn't have done for Mother's sound advice and kind words. In the event the decision was taken out of my hands.

Susanna was a shy girl not used to spilling out her feelings. So the next morning I wasn't surprised when a crumpled little note fell out from under my pillow as I shook out the sheets to make my bed.

Written in tiny neat handwriting were the heart-wrenching words: *Please don't leave Nana.*

Four words that seemed to plunge straight into my chest and envelop my heart.

Clutching the note, I sighed heavily and held it to my face. It smelled of little girls, of perfumed rubbers, ponies and hay. There and then I wanted to fold her into my arms, wrap her up with love and banish her pain for ever.

Children often have a way of simplifying things and getting straight to the heart of an issue. With that one innocent request I knew nothing on earth could make me leave her side. My place now was by Susanna's side and there I must remain until she was ready to leave me.

The instinct and desire to protect a child are all-consuming. Many years later an incident brought this home to me. I was holding a baby when I tripped on a rug. As the floor raced up to reach me I knew the baby would take the impact unless I did something. It was unthinkable that I could fall while holding a baby. Flinging my arm out to take the brunt of the fall, we both landed with a grunt. The baby was quite safe, thank goodness, but I suffered a nasty chipped bone. It was all as instinctive as breathing. My desire to make sure Susanna grew up safe and sound was just as primal as shielding that baby in my arms.

When I went into Susanna's room I knelt down to her level, brushed away a strand of pale blonde hair from her hazel eyes and smiled at her.

'Tell you what. How's about we make some of Nana's famous chocolate cake that you love so much?' I smiled. 'I'll let you lick the bowl out afterwards.'

A shy smile flashed over her little freckled face. 'Yes please,' she said, slipping her tiny hand in mine. Do you know what, to this day that was all that has ever been said on the matter.

I knew she would be mortified if I brought up the note or tried to talk to her about her parents' divorce. Besides, at times like these actions speak louder than words. It's what you *do* that counts, not what you say.

Susanna needed to laugh, eat warm chocolate cake and drink milk as I pottered around the kitchen preparing lunch. Surely that's what childhood should be about? Watching ordinary, everyday events roll out in the knowledge that you are surrounded by love, routine and boundaries.

Mr Gordon sat me down soon after and told me he appreciated my staying on.

'I'll have it written into the divorce papers that you will stay on and provide some continuity of care for Susanna,

217

and I would appreciate you taking over the running of the house,' he said.

The twins were sixteen by then and both lived away from home by that stage, although they visited frequently. Belinda was training to be a riding instructor and Fiona was working too. They were healthy, robust characters and I lived for their visits home. They would burst into the kitchen in a riot of noise, squabbling about something or other that would usually involve me having to untangle them limb by limb.

They were as different from Susanna as chalk and cheese. She was quiet, shy and sensitive and they were . . . well, the twins!

Stripping down Susanna's Barbie doll and tying her to her doll's house was not an uncommon pastime, as were arguing with each other about unsuitable boyfriends and locking Susanna in the tack room at the stables.

They were loud, funny and full of life. I liked them immensely. Watching them now, tugging off riding boots, their wild and curly hair tousled with straw, tussling over who got the strawberry jam out of the fridge first, I marvelled at how much had changed since I had cared for them both as tiny babies back in Kensington.

Mother was long gone, yet these two strapping young girls were hale and hearty. It was life-affirming to watch them now, squabbling and giggling in a cloud of teenage hormones.

'What's for dinner, Nana?' Belinda asked. 'I'm famished.'

Now, up to this point, my culinary expertise was limited. Most of the places I'd worked for had had a cook and I'd been so involved with my babies I'd had no need of the finer points of culinary expertise. Children's palates aren't that sophisticated and boiled eggs and soldiers, cottage pie or meat and two veg followed by a sticky pudding usually sufficed.

'Well,' I stuttered now. 'I could make some omelettes,' I suppose.

'Omelettes?' Belinda laughed.

'Omelettes?' Fiona scoffed, in a rare moment of solidarity. 'Daddy won't accept an omelette for tea. Not when he's been working so hard up at the hospital all day.'

Mrs Gordon was a fine cook and until then had done all the cooking for the house. Now it rather looked as if this would be falling to me.

'Gracious,' I gulped.

'Leave it to me,' said Belinda. 'I'll talk to Daddy.'

She soon returned. Not only had she managed to secure me a pay rise of an extra £5 a week, but Mr Gordon had agreed to send me on a cookery course.

Marjorie Wilton's Cordon Bleu Cookery School in Epsom was like stepping back in time. It may have been the 1970s. The decade when women burnt their bras and the Women's Liberation Movement took to the streets and marched for women's rights or threw flour bombs at the Miss World contest in protest, but right here in leafy Surrey the thing uppermost on women's minds was learning how to make the perfect chicken suprême to serve up to their husband for dinner after he'd returned home on the commuter train.

Surrey in the 1970s was full of women who fancied themselves as Margo in *The Good Life*, and knowing how to make the perfect mushroom vol-au-vents or celery and prawn savouries to serve at your supper party was all the rage. A number of good things came out of the 1970s. The Queen's Silver Jubilee, heart monitors for babies, free contraception, Child Benefit and microwaves to name but a few, but Marjorie's chicken suprême ruled the roost round these parts.

Still, I enjoyed these lessons and to my delight and surprise found myself rather good at cooking. I suppose on the face of it I must have looked like another keen house-wife eager to brush up on her cooking skills, not a nanny being paid to learn to cook for a newly divorced surgeon, but families come in all shapes and sizes, as I was rapidly learning. Not that I minded in any case. I was being paid to learn a new skill and what's better than that?

The assembled housewives and myself oohed and aahed as our teacher taught us to cook fancy dishes that I'd never heard of or seen before. My repertoire, like that of my mother's generation, was basic – good old-fashioned roasts, puddings and pies – plus we had lived through the lean war years, when we'd had to stretch, ration, make do and substitute. I'd practically lived off powdered-egg dishes and meals bulked out with endless potatoes and carrots during the war and postwar years.

Now I was being shown such wondrous dishes as vichy-ssoise, super sausage supper, seafood pancakes, stuffed cheesy courgettes, vegetable medleys, macaroons, soufflé au fromage, prawn cocktail, Black Forest gateau, pineapple homage and tarragon chicken with grapes. It was all quite marvellous.

All the recipes had exotic or foreign names or, failing that, were prefixed with the words 'super' or 'supreme', quite why I don't know, but it certainly made them sound more impressive. Chicken suprême certainly invites more confidence than chicken with a cream sauce, doesn't it? And doesn't a vegetable medley sound better than a plate of vegetables? And whoever thought of teaming duck with orange or chicken with grapes. It heralded a new era of sophistication.

Anyway, the other Surrey housewives and I lapped this up and on the last day our enthusiastic teacher had a treat in store for us.

'Now ladies,' boomed Marjorie, clasping her hands to her generous bosom. 'You are in for a treat. Today I am going to show you how to make *boeuf en croute*.'

Blank faces all round and Marjorie looked a trifle cross.

'Fillet steak in pastry,' she snapped.

'Aaah,' cooed the assembled ladies.

Pleased she had her attentive audience back on form, she went on: 'And for dessert you will be able to amaze and delight your husbands with Marjorie's very own pear mountain.'

More gasps of delight as eyes widened and the ladies imagined how impressed their families would be by a dessert named after something as majestic as a mountain.

Pear mountain indeed. As he was a keen skier, I knew Mr Gordon would be thrilled with a pudding such as this.

What a joy these dishes were to assemble.

As I and the good housewives of Surrey fried delicate fillet steak in beef dripping and sautéed porcini mushrooms in butter, the room was quickly filled with delicious cooking smells. I suppressed a chuckle as I thought what the villagers of Little Cranford where I had worked during some of the war years would have made of this feast. Cordon bleu cookery hadn't even been heard of back then! Those game villagers had 'feasted' on anything they could get their hands on, from rabbits to pigeon and even road-kill. Fillet steak was an unimagined luxury, never mind when slathered with mouth-wateringly rich mushrooms, encased in puff pastry and baked until golden brown and delicious.

As I sliced into the flaky pastry and watched the unctuous beef and mushroom juices ooze out, I knew Mr Gordon was in for a treat.

But the pear mountain was the pièce de résistance.

You simply piled up meringue and cream in a pyramid, then gently placed slices of poached pear around the sides until it was, well, a pear mountain. Next you dribbled hot chocolate sauce over the top of the mountain until it dried to a hard chocolate coating covering the summit.

When I broke through the chocolate shell into the moist pears and creamy-crunchy meringue underneath I felt I'd died and gone to food heaven. Why, I could hardly wait to try out my new-found culinary skills on Mr Gordon. I'd show him how I'd moved on from cottage pie.

Back at home I carefully prepared the dishes I'd learned, starting with *boeuf en croute* and Marjorie's famous pear mountain.

Little Susanna watched me curiously as I mashed, blended, rolled, sautéed and chopped. All children adore cooking, so I let her help me roll out the puff pastry and assemble the pears.

The rich cooking smells soon tempted Mr Gordon from his office. When I placed the dishes on the elegant dining table, he was quite clearly lost for words.

I watched through a crack in the door as he sliced off a piece of the *boeuf en croute* and tasted the rich and buttery dish. His eyes closed and he groaned a little. The plate of food was finished in a matter of moments. A deep sigh of satisfaction escaped his lips when he cracked through the chocolate shell of my pear mountain and spooned a generous helping of chocolate and meringue into his mouth. A look of ecstasy flickered over his face as devoured the pudding.

After he was finished and the plate scraped clean, he loosened his trousers and leaned back in his dining-room chair with a happy groan.

That was money well spent then, I thought happily.

As I collected the empty plates, I smiled brightly at Mr Gordon.

'Very good, Nana.' He smiled gratefully. 'I think we'll be having that pear mountain again.'

Shortly afterwards, Mr Gordon announced his intention to have a dinner party for some of his smart colleagues from the hospital.

'Do that thing, won't you, Nana?' he muttered.

'What's that, Mr Gordon?'

'Oh you know, that *boeuf* thing.'

Mr Gordon was clearly out to impress as he also requested the pear mountain and I caught him going through his beloved wine collection and decanting a dusty bottle of red that even to the untrained eye looked expensive and rare.

The dinner party was a roaring success.

'I say, Daniel,' said one of his well-spoken guests. 'This food is frightfully good. Have you a new cook?'

'No,' Mr Gordon was forced to confess. 'Actually it's Susanna's nanny.'

The guests were obviously impressed at their colleague's thrift in getting a nanny who could double up as a cook.

Before long I found myself catering for these dinner parties on quite a regular basis and I quickly learned that there were two kinds of dinner parties. There were the *boeuf en croute*, pear mountain parties and the plonk parties.

The *boeuf en croute* parties were for his smarter guests, people Mr Gordon felt were on a level with him and could discuss his love of fine wines and skiing. Those people got pear mountain and vintage wines.

His other friends, whom he didn't feel quite up to his level intellectually, got chicken suprême and plonk, by which I mean any old wine.

I knew which type fell into which category quite simply.

'Is it a pear mountain crowd tonight?' I would ask.

'No, Nana,' he'd reply. 'Just a plonk night.'

This amused me no end, though some of the plonk crowd were quite rude and seemed to treat me as if I were just a member of staff or a daily and barely flicked a glance in my direction, much less gave me a thank-you when I placed a plate of food in front of them. Some of them, the women especially, were really quite snooty.

One, a brassy blonde with a loud, braying voice, really got my goat. I knew that now Mr Gordon was single and back on the market he was viewed as a very eligible man. The stream of babbling women who passed through our doors were all keen to become the new Mrs Gordon. Their intentions were as obvious as the jewels glinting round their necks and their hard red lips would be set in a thin line of determination as they got their 'prey' in their sights.

This one in particular laughed outrageously whenever Mr Gordon spoke and hung on his every word. I saw her hard eyes narrow and glare at me suspiciously as I served dinner. They seemed to be saying one thing only: 'Hands off, he's mine.'

I felt like laughing and saying, 'You're in the plonk dinner party, young lady, you don't stand a chance.'

Mr Gordon was like most men in his fifties and appeared to have a burgeoning interest in the opposite sex. I can't say I blamed him. He wanted an attractive wife, and as a well-respected, wealthy surgeon he was quite the catch.

I viewed these comings and goings as an amused bystander. I said nothing, just kept serving up the *boeuf en croute* with a wry grin on my face. Besides, what did it matter, so long as Susanna was loved? She was growing up to be a splendid girl and was potty about her ponies. She and her best friend Nicky lived and breathed them, and I kept the house and tried my hardest to provide stability, love and reassurance for all its occupants.

When Susanna wasn't riding or at school and I wasn't doing housework we would have such fun, tramping through the fields and walking the dog in all weathers. My mantra of fresh air whatever the weather, so heartily instilled during my training, had remained with me.

In keeping with most of her contemporaries, Susanna had to have her adenoids and tonsils out, even though there was nothing wrong with them.

'I don't see why I have to,' she grumbled to her father. But as he was a surgeon she stood no chance and in due course they were whipped out. When she returned, the poor little thing looked white as a sheet.

'Come on,' I said, helping to pull her off the sofa. 'A walk in the fresh air will do you good.'

'It's bitterly cold, Nana,' she grumbled as we made our way across the fields.

'Nonsense,' I scoffed. 'It's spring. Look, the catkins are out.'

But even I had to admit the poor little mite was shivering by the time we returned home. Fixing her some hot buttered toast and honey and wrapping her in a warm blanket seemed to cheer her up no end.

'Perhaps some of your chocolate cake might help too, Nana,' she ventured, wiping dribbles of hot butter off her chin.

I chuckled. How could I deny her anything?

Mind you, the cold never stopped her getting out on her pony Honeysuckle at every opportunity.

Honeysuckle was a pretty little thing, but quite the naughtiest pony you ever came across. All too often Susanna would come in covered in mud from top to toe after Honeysuckle had bucked her off.

It meant so much to Susanna that I show an interest in her passions and immerse myself in her life. For that reason I seemed to spend no end of time polishing and cleaning the tack and sitting on the edges of freezing fields watching her compete in horse shows. My numb fingers and red nose would vanish in an instant, though, as soon as I saw her and Honeysuckle trot out into the field. The stab of pride I felt seeing her sitting up smartly in her gleaming saddle gave me a little lump in my throat and made me feel ten foot tall.

One day, Susanna and Nicky persuaded me to go down to the fields with them, and so, packing a flask of piping-hot pearl-barley soup to keep out the chill, we all went down to the stables. Nicky was just as confident a rider as Susanna, but once there I could see she was a little nervous about riding frisky Honeysuckle.

'I'm not sure,' she ventured. 'You're always coming off him,' she trembled.

'Oh go on, Nicky,' said Susanna.

'What do you think, Nana?' asked Nicky.

'Why not try, dear? I'm sure you'll be brilliant. Better to have given it a go,' I said.

I so passionately believe that children must be allowed to give things a go. What lessons are we teaching them if we say it's OK to shy away from your fears? Nurse Nina Baker summed it up well when she wrote in the Norland newsletter:

Children should certainly be watched and guided when necessary, but always without realising it, so that they are allowed to have a life of their own.

Nowadays 'Fear' is often instilled into children from the beginning because they are seldom allowed to climb a tree or even to climb on to a wall, just in case they fall. How ever are they to learn anything but the thought of danger if they are continually told they mustn't do this and that in case . . . ? A child goes to the dentist and doctor, why suggest that the unfortunate individuals are going to hurt the child, immediately giving the suggestion of fear and uneasiness?

Wise words. And so I shouldn't instil fear in young Nicky before she had even got in the saddle.

'I'm sure you'll be just fine,' I grinned.

'Oh well, if you say so, Nana,' she said. And with that she swung her leg over the saddle. No sooner was she seated than a mischievous gleam appeared in Honeysuckle's big brown eyes. Uh oh. Honeysuckle's ears flattened down against her head and she started to dance around the fields.

'I think she may be getting ready to—' I warned.

Too late. Honeysuckle was already rearing into the air before flicking her back legs up indignantly. The speed with which poor Nicky was bucked off was impressive. One could virtually hear the breath leaving her body as she landed with a spectacular thud on the ground. I remember thinking later, as I gently bathed Nicky's cuts and bruises, that for a small horse she could certainly move like lightning.

'I'm so sorry,' I apologised to Nicky's mother when she collected her. 'I don't think she damaged her head.'

I'm pleased to say that little Nicky is now a lovely young lady and a GP, so I don't think she suffered any lasting damage.

I'm glad I didn't wrap Susanna or Nicky in cotton wool – nor any of my other charges in fact. It's vitally important for young people's self-esteem to allow them to get out and about and into scrapes, to find their own way in the world without filling them with fear about what might happen. In some ways I think it's important that we do almost come a cropper from time to time.

When I was younger I was forever rampaging through bushes and fields and always had cuts on my knees, and when I was working as a sixteen-year-old mother's help I had a similar experience to young Nicky. I'd been out for a riding lesson on a magnificent horse called Jet.

Jet, like Honeysuckle, had the devil in him and decided to take off with me at top speed. Calamity was averted when I managed to stop him just before we shot into a busy road. My brush with death was thrilling, and certainly sent my pulse racing, but it also taught me an important lesson. It taught me that there are no second chances in life and we must grab all that is offered. It was shortly after grappling with the runaway horse that I decided to apply to be a Norland Nanny and the rest is history. Though as I now know from experience, when it comes to dealing with a headstrong horse and a headstrong child, there is often little in it.

The world turns on tiny things and all events, even those that seem terrifying or disastrous, can shape our lives in ways we cannot even imagine. We must embrace all experiences, good and bad, and stay open and positive to everything.

It was such a joy to watch Susanna's personality emerge and her self-esteem and sense of mischief flourish. One dark winter's day, when it was too cold to ride her pony, I was bringing some washing upstairs when she bounded up to me and gripped my arm, her hazel eyes sparkling.

'I've made a ghost-train game. Are you brave enough to take part, Nana?' she laughed.

'A ghost train indeed?' I smiled. 'Well, why not?'

With that she flicked off the landing lights and we were plunged into darkness. I felt her little hand in mine, guiding me across the landing. 'Watch out for the toy ponies, darling,' I warned. At any given time Susanna's plastic toy ponies and jumps were spread all over the floor and I usually had to clear them up in a hurry before Mr Gordon got back from the hospital. It wouldn't do to have one of the country's leading surgeons hopping about with a plastic horse embedded in his heel.

'I should warn you, Susanna, it takes a lot to scare me,' I chuckled. When you've run through the night from German bombers or watched V-1s streak overhead you don't get scared by much.

'Aaah, but you haven't experienced my ghost train, Nana,' her voice rang out in the darkness.

I had to laugh. All children bar none seem to adore being terrified of the dark. When the lights are switched off their senses seem to spiral out of control. A creak on the landing suddenly becomes a terrifying ghoul; a breath of wind on the windowpane a ghost whispering in their ear. I was the same I'm quite sure. In fact, when I was eighteen, training with the Norland at a big old stately home in the heart of the Kent countryside, the blackouts meant that I and the rest of my set spent every night in a chilly attic so cold and dark it was like being underground. Only the hooting of an owl or a baby's soft cry seemed to penetrate the velvety-thick black of the night. We'd spin fantastical ghost stories until we fell asleep huddled together, frightened out of our wits. Half the fun was in being scared!

With that in mind, I shivered for dramatic effect and decided to play along.

'This is terrifying, Susanna. You will take care of me, sweetheart, won't you?' I quivered.

'Don't worry, Nana, I'll protect you,' whispered her voice in the dark. 'Watch out for the witch's hair,' she said as she guided me down the corridor. 'Touch it at your peril.'

'Ooh,' I squealed as I stroked what was obviously my feather duster. 'That's so frightening.'

'Now, Nana, do you dare put your hand here?' she said in a voice thick with mystery. Seconds later I found my hand being plunged into something cold, slimy and wet.

So that's where my plum tomatoes had gone!

'A human eye,' she whispered.

'Bloodthirsty,' I agreed.

An almighty crash rang out as I stumbled over a carefully arranged stack of my best saucepans.

'Lightning,' she shrieked in glee. 'You've disturbed the witch's lair, Nana.'

'Oh no,' I gulped, frantically trying to steady myself against the wall.

Finally, the door to her bedroom creaked and I felt myself being directed in.

'You go first Nana,' she said. 'But beware . . .'

'Of what?' I started to ask, but my voice was drowned out by a loud, soggy splat.

'Arghhh,' I screeched, this time for real. Something soft, damp and wet had landed on my head and was sliding slowly down the side of my face.

Scrabbling for the light switch, I flicked it on to find Susanna on the ground in helpless fits of laughter.

'Your face, Nana,' she giggled as a droplet of water hung off the end of my nose. A damp sponge that had obviously been balanced precariously on the door frame, designed to topple off on to whoever opened the door first, lay discarded by my feet.

'You rotter,' I laughed. Many people might have scolded a child for such a harmless act of mischief, but what would have been the point of that? To suppress the sense of mischief in a child's life is to crush the joy out of them.

Besides, childhood should be full of messy, wet adventures, bruised knees and tricks. Not sure I'd relish being ambushed in the dark with something warm and wet again, mind you!

When she wasn't dropping soggy sponges on her Nana's head, Susanna, like most children her age, was privileged to be part of that new era of children brought up on television. Not just any old television, but colour television programmes specifically made with children in mind. This was unheard of when I was growing up. In my day we had listened to the wireless along with my parents, but even that had usually been just for big events, like the King's coronation.

Mostly for entertainment we used to get round the piano every Sunday night after tea and sing along while my mother played. But nowadays children had *Trumpton*, *Camberwick Green*, *the Flowerpot Men*, *The Magic Roundabout*, and Susanna's favourite *Hector's House*. She named her beloved cat Kiki after one of the animals.

I'm afraid I drew the line at *Dr Who*, though, especially when I saw a terrifying Dalek gliding down a corridor. I nearly jumped out of my skin when I heard their robotic voices. 'We will exterminate . . . we will exterminate.'

'Oh no you won't,' I said, snapping off the television.

A great howl of protest went up. 'Oh Nana, please let me watch it,' pleaded Susanna.

'It will give you nightmares,' I said firmly.

Perhaps I sound overprotective and you would argue it was just innocent fun. I suppose in many ways it was innocent compared to what's on television now, but you have to remember that this was all new for us. I was brought up on sing-songs round the piano and Enid Blyton. A powerful race of extraterrestrial mutants hell-bent on world domination was a bit too rich for me.

Besides, I liked it best when the television was switched off after supper on Saturday evenings and we played snap or Susanna played with her toy horses while I simply sat and sewed or knitted, in quiet companionship. There is a certain magic in the ordinariness of everyday life.

But the genteel peace and quiet of the countryside was shattered one night in a drama so terrifying it ripped me straight back forty years to the heart-stopping horror of the Blitz.

The night began like any other. After a peaceful evening darning while Susanna played with her toy horses on the carpet by my feet I started the evening routine. Bedtime was at 7.30 p.m. prompt, never earlier, never later, and I never gave in, no matter how loud her protestations grew. If you know one thing about me by now, dear reader, it's that I'm a stickler for routine. Children thrive on it and adults should live by it.

After a teeth-clean and a story, I tucked Susanna up under her eiderdown.

'There,' I smiled, pulling the covers tight around her feet to keep them toasty warm, like my own mother had done all those years before. 'You're as snug as a bug in a rug.'

She wriggled in under her covers until just the tip of her freckled button nose peeked out over the top.

'Night night, Nana,' she mumbled sleepily, those dreamy hazel eyes already starting to flicker shut into a delicious sleep.

Kiki then leaped on to her bed. I smiled and shook my head in amazement as she took up her place by Susanna's head and did what she did every night.

Curling her long feline body around Susanna's head and shoulders, Kiki stretched, yawned and settled down. Cats are amazing, but this one was truly extraordinary. She would settle herself down on Susanna's pillow, snuggling into her soft blonde hair until she was fast asleep, like a feline comfort blanket, and then she would softly pad down to the end of the bed to her feet, were she would remain until morning.

I'll confess, I was a bit alarmed when I first saw it, but after a while I began to realise that an instinctive understanding ran between them and that it was their own special routine. Kiki couldn't rest until Susanna was fast asleep and Susanna couldn't sleep until Kiki's soft body was wrapped around her.

Now, Kiki's gentle purrs filled the bedroom as Susanna's breathing grew heavier.

'Night night, my angels,' I chuckled as I switched out the light. 'Sleep tight.'

Softly opening the door that connected my room to Susanna's, I began to make my own preparations for bed.

Goodness knows how long I'd been asleep when a strange noise dragged me from my dreams.

Kiki was frantically batting my head with her paw and yowling at the top of her voice.

'Oh Kiki,' I said crossly. 'Whatever are you doing? Hush now, you'll wake the whole house.'

Blearily I rolled over and groaned when I registered the time on my bedside clock: 3.30 a.m. No person should have to see this time of the night. It had been a long time since I'd been dragged from my sleep at such an ungodly hour and then it was usually by a crying, hungry baby, not a demanding cat.

I reached out to stroke Kiki, but she leaped back, fixed me with her big eyes and yowled at the top of her voice. Every hair on her body seemed to be standing on end as she frantically pawed at the covers.

Slowly it dawned on me. Kiki was trying to tell me something.

'What is it, girl?' I murmured.

Suddenly, at a deep level, my senses became aware of something. I sniffed the air. *Smoke!*

A deep prickle of fear ran the length of my spine and I sat bolt upright in bed. Now I was wide awake. I sniffed again and yes, there it was, that unmistakeable acrid stench that comes with fire.

There wasn't a moment to waste.

Throwing back the covers, I leaped out of bed and frantically pulled on my day dress and shoes. Tearing down the stairs, I realised my heart was thundering in my chest. I knew moments like this were vital. What one did now could make all the difference to our safety.

I followed my nose into the drawing room. There was an open fire there that Mr Gordon liked to light in the evenings and read his paper beside. Perhaps a spark had leaped from the fire and landed on the rug?

But when I nervously pushed open the door everything was still, dark and quiet.

Whirling round, I ran down the passage to the kitchen, yanked open the door and an involuntary gasp left my lips.

There was a passageway that led from the kitchen to the garage. Over the garage there was a flat where a young handyman lived. The passage was already filled with a thick, grey, choking smoke, its deadly vapours suffocating in the small passageway. I glanced up and froze. Terror sliced through my veins.

'Oh my,' I gasped as my hand flew to my mouth.

The ceiling of the passageway was lit up with an eerie orange glow. The fire was obviously up in the flat and its heat was already burning through the floor. It burned the same molten red that I had seen in September 1940. In that instant I was transported back almost forty years to the horrifying moment I had witnessed London engulfed by fire during the Blitz.

I'd been working in my first job in Surrey and had been on my way home to visit Mother on a gusty but clear autumn evening when I'd come across a small crowd of people huddled together in a field.

The field was on top of a hill and everyone was staring spellbound at the view. When I'd reached them I'd turned to see what had captivated them so and all too soon I was dumbstruck.

The landscape surrounding the village was so flat you could often see the lights of London twinkling in the distance. Those same lights had now been replaced by a ferocious orange glow. Eighteen miles away flames billowed into the clear night air.

Not a soul amongst us stirred; we just stood rooted to the spot looking at the terrible sight unfolding before us. No one dared voice it, but we were all thinking one thought. How many people were fighting for their lives in those flames? So many, many courageous souls battled for survival as German bombers filled the skies and unleashed their terrible cargo.

Back then the effect of those flames had been almost hypnotic and now, staring at the same intense glow, I could almost taste the smoke of the Blitz. Rooted to the spot, I closed my eyes and steadied myself against the wall.

Suddenly the same survival spirit kicked in. My life and those of my charges had been in danger many times during the war – and now it was happening again. This was a time for action, not reflection.

Susanna's life depended on it.

'Fire,' I hollered. Then louder: 'FIRE!'

I was about to race up the stairs when a dreadful thought occurred to me. The fire was smack bang above the garage. When it burnt through the ceiling, which it would surely do, the burning wood would fall straight on to the cars below. Fire on cars' full petrol tanks. The effects would be catastrophic. We would all be blown to pieces.

There wasn't a moment to lose. Wild terror pumped through my veins as I raced to the kitchen, grabbed my keys from the hook and then yanked open the connecting door to the garage.

Already I could see the deadly smoke curling and winding its way through the cracks like snakes. As I pushed open the garage door, the cold night air rushed in to meet me. Gratefully sucking the clean air into my lungs, I turned and headed back into the smoky garage.

My hands fumbled as I tried to get the keys in the car door.

Please don't let the ceiling collapse on me. Please.

The car engine roared into life and as I drove out of the garage I could make out the dark figure of Mr Gordon.

'You have to get your car out – quick,' I yelled as I bumped past him. I drove the car as far as I dared and parked it in a neighbouring field, then, without pausing for breath, I turned and tore back across the fields. Susanna, Susanna, I had to get her. *Please don't let me be too late.* By now the flat was ablaze, flames billowing out of the window.

The handyman stood dazed and sooty outside the house, staring at his burning flat.

'Call the fire brigade,' I yelled as I ran past him.

Bursting through the open front door, I took the stairs two at a time. Susanna was just as I had left her. Fast asleep in her bed, her chest gently rising and falling. Thank goodness.

Grabbing a handful of clothes from her wardrobe, I turned to her and scooped her out of bed.

'Nana,' she mumbled sleepily. 'What's going on?'

'I'll explain in a bit, sweetheart. We've got to get out.'

Clutching her to my chest, I staggered down the stairs. Once outside in the cold night I gasped great lungfuls of fresh air.

Mr Gordon had grabbed a ladder and a hose and was showering the fire with water. Great plumes of thick grey smoke pumped out over him. It was a brave thing to do and I stood aghast, watching him through the clouds of smoke.

'Get Susanna to the car,' he yelled.

As I turned and ran to the safety of the car, Susanna's body stiffened in mine.

'Honeysuckle,' she yelled.

'She's fine,' I soothed. 'Her stables are far enough away.'

'Lulu,' she cried.

Lulu the dog was a precious member of the family. I couldn't leave her in there. Placing Susanna in the car, I passed over her clothes, which I only now realised were her school clothes.

'Put these on, sweetheart, and don't move,' I ordered. 'I'll be back soon.'

'I must be mad,' I puffed as I raced back into the house. The fire seemed to be out by now, but the house was fast filling with fumes. I knew I didn't have long.

Fortunately Lulu was curled up and whimpering in her basket. 'Come with me,' I soothed, gently lifting her body into my arms.

By the time I got outside the fire brigade had screeched to a halt and had already swung into action. In no time at all the fire was out.

As the firemen secured the house, Susanna ventured from the car. Mr Gordon, Susanna, myself and the handy-man stood stock-still in the driveway, staring at the shell that had once been the garage and flat.

What a sorry sight we made. Susanna in her dishevelled school clothes, Mr Gordon with his face as black as soot and me, a bedraggled mess.

'Well,' I exclaimed finally. 'What a night. Who wants a cup of tea?'

As I bustled round serving tea and biscuits to Mr Gordon and the fire crew my gaze fell on the young handyman, slumped on the floor with his head in his hands.

Poor man. He'd lost everything.

'The electric blanket,' he whispered with a face as white as flour. 'I thought I'd turned it off.'

Just then a flash of black and white caught my eye.

'Well,' I declared, shaking my head in amazement as a ball of sooty fur burst down the path and into Susanna's outstretched arms.

'Here comes the heroine of the hour.'

Kiki was curled up and purring in her arms as Susanna kissed and nuzzled her head over and over.

'If it hadn't been for that cat I fear the very worst would have happened to us,' I whispered.

Dawn was creeping in over the horizon by the time we all made it back to bed, exhausted.

Nowadays a shrieking smoke alarm would have wrenched us from our sleep, but back then, thank goodness, we'd had the good fortune to live with that cleverest, most insightful and resourceful of creatures: a cat. Kiki the feline firefighter really was our very own lifesaver that night.

After the drama of the fire had died down and the garage was repaired, life settled back into a comfortable routine.

It was wonderful to watch Susanna's childhood gently

roll out and see her blossom into a teenager. It was an innocent, joyful time, filled with mud-spattered adventures and plenty of fresh air, good food and love. A childhood in the most proper sense of the word, untouched by adult ways, in which she was not forced to grow up too soon. Her parents may have parted, but I hoped I'd done my best to shield her from the worst of it and keep her childhood as innocent as possible.

I also enjoyed hearing about the childhoods of my fellow Norland Nurses. Nurse Baker wrote in the newsletter about her own adventurous upbringing:

When I was small, our supply of toys was limited, but well thought out. When we built anything we were allowed to leave it up for any length of time we wished. To me this is most important from a psychological point of view. I often wonder how adults would feel if they made anything with great care and were then ordered to pull it to pieces because it was bedtime, mealtime or something else.

The garden was ours to use as we liked. We dug large holes and had a wonderful wooden hut, made by ourselves with a real sacking roof and coated with tar. There we cooked on a fire, all made in a bucket such as we saw the watchman in the road use.

Our cooking utensils were a biscuit-tin lid for a frying pan and tins for water. In our improvised frying pan we cooked bacon and chips, and we usually had sixpence each to buy what we liked to add to the feast, which more often than not was ginger beer or apples. In our hut we experimented making gas in a football bladder, and probably nearly blew ourselves up, but we didn't and nobody appeared worried. We also made fires by making a hole in the earth and building up around the hole with bricks and then baked our potatoes actually in the hole amongst the ashes.

Many a time we climbed out of bedroom windows at night to collect stag beetles from the ivy. To climb to the roof of the house via the drainpipes was a mere nothing and again nobody worried. We experimented with anything and everything, including making fountains from the bathroom tap. We built museums and went miles to add to our flint and butterfly or birds' egg collections. I was not a strong child and there was very little to spare for luxuries, but my two brothers and I were allowed freedom to experiment and enjoy our independence.

I blush now to think of some of the things we did – such as climbing out of the playroom window over to the bedroom window to frighten our poor unfortunate nurse while she was dressing. We were never smacked but we were allowed to have no fads whatsoever.

I love this account of a Norlander's childhood because it was similar to my own, albeit slightly more adventurous. It just goes to show, if you give children the freedom to enjoy their childhood, make mistakes and enjoy simple outdoor pursuits, they will grow up to be sensible, well-adjusted adults.

Except that children in the 70s had the kind of relationships with their elders that I could only have imagined. Children weren't just confined to day and night nurseries, rolled out to meet their parents at the hour after tea, trussed up in corsets and trotted out in crocodile lines to church like I had been.

They could watch television programmes while munching toast and honey on their laps, interact with their teachers, have a say in their futures. In the 1960s and now definitely in the 70s children could be both seen *and* heard.

I so ardently hoped that I had done my best to give Susanna the kind of childhood I knew she deserved.

They were blissful times and with a jolt, in 1980, I realised I had been with the Gordons for fifteen years. A little longer than the six weeks I had planned on staying.

I hadn't kept in touch with any of my fellow Norlanders, but I had heard that many now worked abroad for wealthy families. A private nanny was still in demand, as well I knew, but only if you had the means to afford it.

The face of childcare had changed beyond all measure since I had trained so fastidiously in Pembridge Square in 1939. Now mothers employed cheap, untrained help in the form of au pairs. In 1962 the Preschool Playgroups Association for under-fives had been formed with the intention of providing cheap, reliable childcare for mothers wishing to return to work, but also to highlight to the government the importance of preschool provisions.

I had smiled proudly at this news. I had worked in one of the forerunners to this – the war nurseries set up so that mothers could do their bit for the war effort, content in the knowledge that their children were safely cared for. I liked to think I had done my bit and that now, in 1980, thanks to the efforts of all of us who had worked in the nurseries, state nurseries, crèches and playgroups were freeing women to work and follow their hearts.

What good was it having equal pay, employment protection and sex discrimination acts protecting women at work if they had nowhere to leave their children?

But I realised, too, that something else more powerful and life-affirming than any of those events had happened in the last fifteen years, at least in my life. I had finally put down roots. I had stayed and helped to raise Susanna through her most important years and for one simple reason. Love.

Love had found me and I had found love, maybe not with a man, but in a relationship infinitely more powerful and a hundred times more rewarding: *with a child*. Not my flesh and blood, but my daughter all the same.

Finally, after all these years, after losing my parents, I had found the closest thing to a family to call my own. My mission was over. I had come home.

Soon after, Mr Gordon found his new wife. A lovely young beautician whom he seemed quite taken with. History doesn't recount whether she was in the plonk dinner party or the pear mountain dinner party, but he was happy and that was what counted.

At more or less the same time Susanna went off to start her new life at boarding school. She was excited and seemed happy to be going and I shared in her excitement. She was leaving me, not me leaving her, and that's the proper way of things with children.

Mr Gordon didn't seem too pleased when I informed him that I too would be taking my leave. I sat nervously opposite him in his study. Kiki seemed to sense my anxiety and wove around my legs, purring softly.

'It's time for me to move on,' I whispered. 'Sorry, Mr Gordon.'

Smiling sadly I reached down and gently tugged Kiki's ears. She responded by leaping into my lap and nuzzling my neck like she had night after night with Susanna. 'Sorry, girl,' I soothed, feeling comfort from the tickle of her soft fur against my skin. 'I know you'll look after Mr Gordon now.'

'It's not my will, Nana,' Mr Gordon said quietly. But it was mine. I knew all too well that having two ladies in the house caring for one man simply wouldn't work. It wasn't fair on his new wife. This was her house to run now.

Saying goodbye to Mr Gordon was a wrench. He could be a little gruff at times but he was also an immensely kind, gentle and loyal man and over the years he and I had been on quite a rollercoaster together. From death to divorce to house fires, our relationship had weathered many storms and I admired and respected him enormously, but he had a new life now.

Besides, with Susanna gone, my work was done. Still, although we no longer lived under the same roof our lives were intertwined now, our souls linked by having experienced the same milestones, and I knew I would always be in her life and in her heart, just as she was in mine. And with that simple realisation I went from being a nanny to a parent. I'm not saying I ever replaced her mother in her heart or her affections; I'm pleased to say Susanna always maintained a wonderful bond and relationship with her own mother. Simply that I was there as well, as a surrogate mother.

My door was always open to her when she returned home from school on holidays, I listened to her hopes, her dreams and her anxieties over a slice of her favourite chocolate cake or toast and honey. I was as nervous as she when she took and passed her exams, and had the tissues ready when she suffered a love-life crisis and burst through the doors in floods of tears. I whooped when she got her first job and wept tears of joy as she walked down the aisle to be married.

As I listened to her exchange vows with her new husband, Blaise, and promised to love, honour and obey him, I was reminded of a vow I had taken a long, long time ago. In 1939, as a trembling young recruit, I had promised to uphold the Norland motto: 'Love Never Faileth'.

One hundred children on, I feel I've upheld that vow. Now whenever people ask me, 'What's the key, Brenda? What's the secret to raising happy children?' my answer remains the same. It's really quite simple. *Love, love and more love*. That's what children need.

Testimonials

Nana was my rock. She was always there for me, when I was tiny, when I was growing up and when I was old enough to know better. Never questioning always supporting. Her total love and kindness to me were those of a mother. I never knew any different. And so it has always been and is still now, and the most lovely thing for me is that my children love her just as I have always done. Truly inspirational, with a love of babies that enabled her, even at the age of 80, to get up in the small hours to care for them. She just has a way with them that is impossible to put into words, they just respond to her. 'I can't' is not in her vocabulary. Always there to help and love, through good times and bad.

Susanna Morris

Nana was *always* busy and you never used to see her relax. She was often either doing the sewing or ironing. Nametapes were sewn on perfectly, shoes were always clean and she used to do the most amazing red ribbon bows in Susanna's bunches – parting completely straight of course! What Nana really loved doing best was looking after tiny babies and she was in her element looking after Susanna as she was so tiny when she was born and needed quite a lot of special looking after. She was also wonderful when she came back to look after my two girls (who are now aged 19 and 16) and you always felt completely safe with Nana in charge! She did however manage to trip over a rug that we had in our kitchen (our fault I'm sure for having it there!) whilst she was holding Sophie who had just been born, and instead of dropping her, she fell with her arms still wrapped round Sophie to protect her and landed on her shoulder, chipping a bone. You always knew where you were with Nana as there was never any leeway with her rules and she was a real stickler for routine, particularly with young children and bedtimes, but she mixed it all with lots of love and affection, which I think is the perfect ingredient for a happy family.

Fiona Gibson (one of the twins)

NANNY'S WISDOM

Give children security

All children need consistency and continuity in their lives. It's vitally important in order for them to feel secure, confident, happy and good about themselves. It was very painful for Susanna when her parents divorced and sadly this is not uncommon. Divorce rates seem to be skyrocketing, I'm not sure why, but perhaps this is another good reason why I never actively pursued a relationship.

I'm so glad it was agreed that I stay on to care for Susanna after her parents parted. It meant I could really be there to ensure she didn't suffer. Susanna and I didn't talk about the divorce much, the main thing was I was there, and I could lavish her with love and cuddles whenever I sensed she was down. I think all parents who are going through a divorce could do well to remember that. It's not what they say, it's what they do; it's their actions that count. Families rocked by a break-up need to be fair, reliable, consistent, but above all must physically be there with a ready supply of cuddles and kisses. Painful separations can be soothed if both parents put their children's emotional wellbeing first.

Put black back

Some children do seem to react strongly to colour. Susanna absolutely yelped whenever anyone, even her own father or godmother, came near her wearing a dark-coloured suit. Some babies find dark colours intimidating and frightening. I never wore black, only white, pastels or on occasion royal blue, and I know babies reacted better to it.

Let children be our teachers

Sometimes we adults get so caught up in our obsession to impart wisdom to children that we can forget that children have a lot to teach us too. Throughout my career, even when caring for evacuees and the sick children at Great Ormond Street, I rarely saw children feeling sorry for themselves, and it made me realise how I should take my cues from them. I think we can all learn from children, if we only just stop and listen to the little people in our lives. Their minds are young, uncluttered and unbiased. They see things very simply and without prejudice – surely the perfect way to approach any situation in life?

Afterword

Love, Love and More Love
2013, Aged 92

> Star light, star bright,
> The first star I see tonight,
> I wish I may, I wish I might,
> Have the wish I wish tonight.
> > Nineteenth-century
> > nursery rhyme

I am eternally grateful for the love that I was able to give to and in return receive from Susanna and her family. We don't share blood, but a powerful, all-consuming love flows through my veins for her.

After Susanna went to boarding school I carried on working until well into my seventies, when I finally retired. Not once did I lose my enthusiasm or my total devotion and love for the job. Why don't you retire? my brothers gasped when I turned seventy. Why? I shrugged. Being a nanny wasn't a job as far as I was concerned. It was my vocation, my calling, and everyone knows you can't simply retire from love. Children leave you; you don't leave children. That's the natural order of things. As long as I had breath in my body and the will to go on I would.

The fresh, unlined face that I started with aged eighteen, grew more wrinkled over time and my brown curls faded to silver. But each laughter line told a story; the creases round my eyes were deep furrows from years of laughter spent in the company of children. I'll admit, there were times when my back ached and my knees throbbed. Bending down to a child's level was certainly more of a challenge as the years rolled by, but I ignored the aches and pains because the passion in my heart and the fire in my belly urged me to keep on, day after day, child after child, year after year.

I eventually stopped in my late seventies, and that was because Kathleen had retired as a midwife and then promptly had a breakdown. Poor Kathleen, she always wanted something or somebody to belong to her, but she never found love or had children. Like me, she spent her life in service and so never found the time to have her own family. Unlike me, it affected her deeply and I suspect it led in part to her breakdown.

Kathleen always loved Yorkshire, so I felt it my duty to move with her and keep her company. She was family, after all, and one must put family first. So I retired and we moved into a little bungalow, two elderly spinsters together. A nanny and a midwife with about 120 years' experience between them of delivering and caring for babies. Dinner-table conversation certainly did tend to revolve around baby stories.

And that would have been that, the end of the story. Except then Susanna fell pregnant and asked for my help. I was absolutely thrilled to come out of retirement aged eighty to help care for Susanna's two children, Felix in 1999, and then Jemima a year later.

Such joy I didn't know existed. Felix and Jemima are my 'grandcharges', and as every grandparent knows, that is a unique relationship. When I held them in my arms, as I had done all those years before with their mother, I marvelled at the glory of life and birth. My baby had had her babies – what an unbelievably astonishing moment. 'You clever thing, you,' I smiled when she brought them home from hospital.

Just like that I knew I had to go on, and suddenly, with renewed vigour, I became the nanny I had been all those years before, getting up in the night to feed them, pacing the bedroom with Felix when he decided to try out his little lungs or just sitting snuggled with them on my lap.

With each child I stayed for six weeks to help Susanna get back on her feet and then I decided to move back down to the south of England to be closer to them and to my brothers.

That was my last job and perhaps my proudest. Today, Susanna is forty-eight and I love her, care for her and worry about her like you would a daughter. She visits me regularly and she is so good, picking me up and having me to stay at Christmas and Easter. When I was confined to hospital recently after a fall she rushed to my side and told the doctor she was my daughter. What a lovely warm feeling it gave me to hear her say that.

Felix is fourteen and Jemima thirteen and they are both splendid children who regularly have me in fits of giggles. Jemima adores my chocolate cake and cheeky Felix makes me laugh so. Last Christmas we went to church and it was so packed we all had to squeeze into the pew. Felix slid off the end of the pew and pulled a hilarious face when no one was watching. The naughty thing kept nudging me until I had tears streaming down my face. What a scream! His voice is breaking and he seems to grow six inches every time I see him. He towers over me and I'm so proud of the fine young man he's growing into.

Jemima is a beautiful, intelligent, affectionate young lady who is forever giving me cuddles. 'I'm your last baby, aren't I, Nana?' she says all the time. Bless her, she is so terribly proud to be my last charge.

The last time I stayed with them they had picked me the most wonderful bunch of flowers and put them by the side of my bed in a vase. I was so touched. Jemima even wrote me a beautiful poem. They both call me Nana, just as Susanna still does. What a privilege and honour to have earned that name.

Many years ago I read that Prince Rainier III had invested his Norland Nanny Kathleen, whom he also called Nana, with the highest honour in the land for being his constant companion growing up and then going on to care for his nieces and nephews. I marvelled at her devotion in serving two generations of the same family. Well, I'm thrilled that I have now done the same.

Us Norland Nurses are built of stern stuff and are built for longevity. I'm not alone in devoting my life to child-care. One nurse, Dorothy Waters, who has long since passed away, wrote in the *Norland Quarterly* in 1950 of her long and satisfying career:

When I first trained in 1913 I was taught that cleanliness and punctuality were most important in a baby's life, but the most important thing was that a baby must be loved;

without love no baby can thrive. I applied these principles and remained in one post 17 years. My friends and family told me I was ruining my chances in life, but I have proved them wrong. I am thankful I can still enjoy the company of small children, and my temporary posts now give me an immense amount of pleasure, and I have so many happy memories. A small girl falling from her cot on to me in the middle of the night, snuggling down and saying, 'I do love you most fwightfully.' Another small boy saying 'I like you. You've got lots of playingness in you.' At a family lunch party, a cousin the same age as my charge, asked me loudly if I had ever been married. My charge hastily answered, 'No, she hasn't, but she has lots of children.'

And do you know, I feel exactly like Nurse Dorothy! I have a hundred children although I have never given birth. How many women can say that?

Sadly my sister Kathleen and brothers Basil and Michael have passed away, but David, now eighty-three, and Christopher, now eighty-five, are very dear to me. They ring me every Sunday and visit regularly to check I am OK. To me they'll always be my baby brothers.

As for me? Today, I am ninety-two years old and I can look back on a wonderful, rich and rewarding life crammed full of adventures and love.

I've had my heart broken and battered, been betrayed and bombed, but I've kept smiling throughout. Being a nanny is not for the faint-hearted, you know! It's a calling, not a career, that's for certain. But I owe my profession a debt of gratitude. Looking after babies and children has kept the sparkle in my eye and the spring in my step. There has never been a dull moment. Children have moved me from extremes of despair and heartache to sheer joy and helpless giggles.

They say caring for children keeps you young. Perhaps that's why I was able to come out of retirement at eighty years old. I am proud to say I've been a nanny for sixty-two glorious years. Surely that makes me Britain's longest-serving nanny?

I never dreamed when I graduated from the Norland Institute aged eighteen that I'd still be looking after babies aged eighty! Which just goes to show that if your heart is full of love for little children your body will keep on going.

I never did find true love or have a child to call my own. There were simply too many babies who needed my love. Yes, I sacrificed my dreams of finding love and having my own family to care for the offspring of others, but I have not one single regret.

I've seen childcare trends come and go but the only thing any mother need really do is to give her whole heart over to love. If she does this, the rewards will be endless.

In sixty-two years I hope I have imparted a little of that love, magic and wisdom. I am still in touch with many of those children today and every year at Christmas and birthdays I am rewarded with many letters and photos from my 'babies', now all grown-up.

These days my life is a little less eventful. I live in sheltered accommodation and my windows are usually thrown open whatever the weather to ensure a steady stream of fresh air. Once a Norlander, always a Norlander.

I may live alone but I have the memories of a thousand cuddles from chubby arms. Those smiles and the magical sound of a child's laughter will keep me going for a few more years yet.

I dare say as a Norland Nurse I could have worked for royalty or diplomats and travelled the world. But I didn't. I'm proud to say I stayed on British soil and did my duty. It's funny, duty is almost regarded as a dirty word these days, but for me it means being proud to be associated with a cause in which you believe, proud to be in the service of children.

In 1953 our Queen had the responsibilities of a nation placed on her twenty-seven-year-old shoulders when she was crowned in a spectacular coronation in which she promised to be a 'servant to my people'. An onerous promise for one so young. The same year I was awarded my badge of merit from the Norland for more than five years' faithful service to one family. I daresay our duties are a little different, but our intentions are the same.

Today the Queen is eighty-seven and I am ninety-two, and we can each look back on long and happy lives spent in the service of people who depended upon us. Last year she looked back on sixty years of devoted service to her people as we all helped her to celebrate her Diamond Jubilee. I look back on my sixty-two years in the service of children with every bit as much pride and joy. I don't regret a single day or a single precious experience. I like to think I did my little bit to help secure the safety and freedom of our children and I found love by the bucketload along the way.

The Norland motto is 'Love Never Faileth' and I hope I have never failed a single child. More than anything I hope I have lived my life nobly, bravely and with honesty, virtues I hold dear. I never made much money being a nanny, but I don't give two hoots for that. I can't take it with me so what is the point of having a well-stuffed bank account? Instead I have something far, far more valuable – sixty-two years in the service of children, and that, in my opinion, is priceless. Children should be cherished, loved, adored and nurtured every day and at every stage of their lives.

Of course I am now at a stage in my life where I start to reflect on my passing, but I don't fear it; oh no, I know exactly where I am going.

In heaven I will be able to look down and watch over all my babies. Until then I thank each and every one for a truly magical and blessed life.

NANNY'S WISDOM

Nannies hear the funniest things
Sophie, talking to gardener: 'Jimmy, would you like an apple?'
Jimmy: 'No thank you, I haven't any teeth.'
Sophie: 'Nanny, Jimmy hasn't any teeth. Will you lend him yours?'

Lucy: 'You haven't much hair, Daddy, have you?'
Daddy: 'No darling, I'm afraid I haven't.'
Lucy: 'It's all gone sort of phphpht, never mind, you go to Nanny, she'll fix it for you.'

Nanny: 'Please God, send me some patience and send it quickly.'
Sally: 'Doesn't God send you enough patience, Nanny?'

Richard, aged three, was handing round his sweets, called Lifesavers, when he saw the proprietress of the hotel he and his family were staying at occupied cleaning a grate. She answered his offer saying it was too early in the morning for sweets, so Richard replied, 'You better have these, they are lifesavers.'

Susie, aged four: 'Nurse, I know I am eating cow, but am I eating her horns too?'

A five-year-old instructing his younger brother: 'When you die, your body will be put in the churchyard, all except your feet. They will go straight to God.'

Nurse: 'Not your feet, your soul.'
Five-year-old: 'That is just what I was saying; you cannot take your soles off your feet.'

Five-year-old John, standing on a dresser with a bottle in his hand about to empty the contents into a goldfish bowl: 'I am just going to give these little darlings a few drops of Vapex. I could not bear them to catch my cold.'

Five-year-old Frankie: 'Do you know what I should do if I was going to die? I should get lots of string and I should tie it all around my new wheelbarrow and then I should tie it around my waist so when I was caught up to the clouds to meet Jesus, it would simply have to come too.'

An invitation from the publisher

Join us at www.hodder.co.uk, or follow us
on Twitter @hodderbooks to be a part of
our community of people who love the very
best in books and reading.

Whether you want to discover more about a book
or an author, watch trailers and interviews, have the
chance to win early limited editions, or simply browse
our expert readers' selection of the very best books,
we think you'll find what you're looking for.

And if you don't, that's the place to tell us what's missing.

We love what we do, and we'd love you to be a part of it.

www.hodder.co.uk

 @hodderbooks

HodderBooks

HodderBooks